# Michael Ignatieff:
# The Lesser Evil?

Derrick O'Keefe

VERSO

London • New York

First published by Verso 2011
© Derrick O'Keefe 2011

1 3 5 7 9 10 8 6 4 2

**Verso**
UK: 6 Meard Street, London W1F 0EG
US: 20 Jay Street, Suite 1010, Brooklyn, NY 11201
www.versobooks.com

Verso is the imprint of New Left Books

ISBN-13: 978-1-84467-615-6

**British Library Cataloguing in Publication Data**
A catalogue record for this book is available from the British Library

**Library of Congress Cataloging-in-Publication Data**
A catalog record for this book is available from the Library of Congress

Typeset in Minion Pro by MJ Gavan, Cornwall
Printed in the US by Maple Vail

DERRICK O'KEEFE is a Canadian writer, editor and social justice activist based in Vancouver. He is an advisory board member and former editor-in-chief of rabble.ca, a popular website featuring progressive news and analysis. He coauthored Malalai Joya's *A Woman Among Warlords: The Extraordinary Story of an Afghan Who Dared to Raise Her Voice.*

# COUNTERBLASTS

COUNTERBLASTS is a series of short, polemical titles that aims to revive a tradition inaugurated by Puritan and Leveller pamphleteers in the seventeenth century, when, in the words of one of their number, Gerard Winstanley, the old world was "running up like parchment in the fire." From 1640 to 1663, a leading bookseller and publisher, George Thomason, recorded that his collection alone contained over twenty thousand pamphlets. Such polemics reappeared both before and during the French, Russian, Chinese and Cuban revolutions of the last century.

*In a period where politicians, media barons and their ideological hirelings rarely challenge the basis of existing society, it is time to revive the tradition. Verso's Counterblasts will challenge the apologists of Empire and Capital.*

# CONTENTS

# PREFACE

In 1993—in the midst of one of many self-styled re-inventions, this time as a war reporter—Michael Ignatieff drove from Zagreb to Belgrade, filming an episode of his BBC documentary series on nationalism, "Blood and Belonging."

This particular hour-long installment examines the disintegration of Yugoslavia in the wake of the war between the Serbian-controlled central government and the breakaway Croatian republic.

Ignatieff, then at the peak of his renown as a media personality in Britain, narrated the program, alternating cool analytical detachment and bald condescension. At one point, he casually tosses off a line about "the grim second-rate-ness of Balkan life." But it's more than the occasional tone of superiority that irks.

A sophisticated cosmopolitan in uniform—black leather jacket, sunglasses, driving a black convertible—Ignatieff introduces the episode over coffee at an outdoor café in the capital of the new Croatia. He then sets off on the road to Belgrade along the Highway of Brotherhood and Unity, as it was known when it formed the spine of Tito's Yugoslavia. Ignatieff faces no harrowing close calls along the now mostly deserted road, just some encounters with the beleaguered and bitter survivors of the 1991 war.

His first stop is a Serbian enclave, guarded by Jordanian UN troops. After a visit to the remnants of the museum dedicated to the victims who died at the World War II era Ustache concentration camp, he visits a Serbian village leveled to the ground in the more recent carnage. Here, he meets an elderly Serb couple, in their 80s, living "like paupers" in one of the few structures left standing, a dilapidated shed. The couple show Ignatieff their few earthly possessions, and share their stories of woe and steadfastness. We learn that the husband is a survivor of two ethnic cleansings, having escaped the Ustache death camp as a young man. We, the viewers, never learn the couple's names. We never learn about how they feed themselves or how they survive, or whether there are others like them in the vicinity.

Driving eastward along what he derisively calls the Serbo-Croatian "Road to Nowhere," Ignatieff soon hits the frontier Croatian town of Osijek. Here, the cameras follow him on a day of riding around town in a van driven by one Branimir Glavas: "A respectable politician, who just happens to run his own private militia. He's a warlord, which makes him a popular man in a frontier town," intones Ignatieff.

In one shot, we watch as Glavas glad hands with the locals through his open, driver's side window. The camera then pans back to Ignatieff, who, from his spot in the backseat, leans forward like a child excited about talking to the grown-ups in front before gushing: "Everybody seems to know you here, it's unbelievable."

With Ignatieff by his side, Glavas is feted everywhere he goes. At one stop he is even serenaded by a couple of zealous young supporters, "Branimir, the flower of Slavonia / The whole of Osijek is with you." Later, Ignatieff accompanies Glavas to "the frontline"— the demarcation resulting from the 1991 war—where earnest, middle-aged Croats testify to their determination to fight for their homeland. We don't learn many specifics about this local strongman, or about the fighting in 1991, though we are told that Glavas "opposed all conciliation with the Serbs," forming his militia before the formal declaration of Croatian independence.

By May, 2009, both of the men we'd followed along their joyride through the new Croatia had undergone monumental

re-branding. Ignatieff had been through two significant trans-
formations of public personae: first shedding the skin of the war
reporter to become an academic human rights sage enamored
with the exercise of American military might, then trading in the
Stars and Stripes for the much humbler maple leaf, returning to
his native Canada to lead the opposition Liberal Party.

For his part, Branimir Glavas went from being "a respectable
politician" and "the flower of Slavonia" to something much less
flowery, having been found guilty of war crimes by a Croatian court
for the torture and murder of Serb civilians in Osijek. Sentenced to
several years in jail, he fled to Bosnia and Herzegovina, where he
was re-arrested. He managed to avoid extradition to Croatia, but
is now serving an eight-year sentence for war crimes.

The captured, tried, and punished Glavas is a rare case among
the lords of war who have shared Ignatieff's company or who
have benefited from his intellectual efforts over the past couple
of decades. Ignatieff was one of the most influential liberal proponents of the 2003 invasion of Iraq. For George W. Bush, Donald
Rumsfeld, Dick Cheney, Tony Blair, and the rest of those whose
war crimes Ignatieff provided with intellectual justification and
political support, impunity remains the norm—so far not one has
been prosecuted. International law, such as it is, remains something applied to the weak and the defeated; the vast majority of
those responsible for the most egregious war crimes remain free to
publish memoirs and roam the elite lecture circuits.

No doubt that nameless old Serb couple squatting amidst the
ruins of war have both now departed this world. The victims
of war who die of old age are, comparatively at least, the lucky
ones—notwithstanding the heartrending stanza from Canadian
Al Purdy's poem "Small Wars": "there are battles / in which the
dead men look so peaceful / and the living so maimed by death
/ you would think they were the corpses / and found their way
home."[1] The body counts (which the US, in its glorious exception-
alism, boasts that it doesn't engage in) of the wars of the past two
decades are staggering.

For Michael Ignatieff and his cohort of "cruise missile human-itarians," this is all so much unfortunate collateral damage in a noble and necessary venture. They wring their hands so that the war makers don't have to; keep moving the goalposts, so that the public don't see how wide of the target the rationale for war was in the first place. Their affinities are with the powerful of this world. More realistic and serious than the fuzzy-headed liberal pacifist, they know the "frontier zones" must be patrolled and disciplined with violence. Many, like Ignatieff, have been to those untamed zones where, in his words, "barbarians rule," and so can claim to know best what needs to be done.

Both literally and figuratively, Ignatieff has allowed himself to be taken for a ride by war criminals, both small-timers and bigger ones. The difference with Glavas was that Ignatieff knew he was in the backseat—for the most part, he convinces himself that he's the one driving. This unearned, hubristic confidence in his own bearings and sense of direction has led, over the years, to many blunders—the latest being his push for the leadership of the Liberal Party, a job for which he fought so hard and so viciously that he seemingly didn't take the time to consider what he'd do with it once he got it—as one Liberal observer pointed out, he asked only "How," and not "Why?"[2]

The main beneficiaries of Ignatieff's flailing, spectacularly underwhelming turn as Liberal leader have been on Canada's political Right—conservative proponents of war-making and fealty to empire-building. Whatever twists and turns Ignatieff's career has taken, or been taken on, this much, at least, has been consistent.

# INTRODUCTION

*We see our lives in language and thus in representation. We always see through a glass darkly, never face to face. Yet even if the real is hidden, it exists and by inference and patient study, we can make out its shape. Only the most devoted attention to what is real can help us to make judgments and take actions which are both responsible and efficacious. Virtual reality is seductive. We see ourselves as noble warriors and our enemies as despicable tyrants. We see war as a surgical scalpel and not a bloodstained sword. In so doing we mis-describe ourselves as we mis-describe the instruments of death. We need to stay away from such fables of self righteous invulnerability. Only then can we get our hands dirty. Only then can we do what is right.*

Michael Ignatieff concluded *Virtual War*, his book examining NATO's 1999 war against Serbia and its implications, with stark warnings about the delusions of war and its makers. He failed to take his own advice, however, infamously propagandizing in favor of the Iraq War just a few years later, when those who did what Ignatieff had then counseled was "right" ended up with hands that were not so much "dirty" as stained. Nevertheless, a decade on, the real Ignatieff remains largely hidden, as if seen through a glass darkly. It's worth undertaking a patient and detailed study to make out his true shape, so that an efficacious and responsible judgment can be made.

The debates and polemics Ignatieff has engaged in over the past decades—on topics including war and empire, torture, civil liberties in the war on terror, the nature of modern liberalism, the impact of human rights discourse, and the potential for and desirability of societal transformation—remain as relevant as ever. But Ignatieff's career as a politician and public intellectual raises a series of questions. First off, just what was it about politics in Canada that it could countenance a 30-year absence from the country in one of its political leaders? Of more universal application: What exactly is the state of liberalism today? Can imperial wars ever be justified? Were the torture and other murky practices of the "war on terror" necessary as a lesser evil? What are the responsibilities of intellectuals?

Perhaps the most important question raised by Ignatieff's life and work is one which he and his intellectual forebears answer in the negative: Was a truly different politics and better world possible, or were all revolutionary and transformative social and economic projects merely paving the way to hell? If we can answer this question in the affirmative, humanity may yet build a road to a future organized not around choices between contending evils but rather around the complementary goods of freedom, participation, equality, ecological integrity and social justice.

This investigation will proceed roughly chronologically, starting with Ignatieff's childhood as a foreign services brat and his education first at an elite private boarding school, then at the Universities of Toronto and Harvard. The scion of an aristocratic Russian family, Ignatieff was brought up in comfort and privilege. His great grandfather was a czarist Minister of Interior; his grandfather, the last czar's Minister of Education, barely escaped execution at the hands of the Bolsheviks before taking the family into exile, first in Britain and then in Canada. His father, George Ignatieff, a close associate of Nobel Peace Prize winner Prime Minister Lester "Mike" Pearson, represented the family's adoptive country as a diplomat and ambassador. On his mother's side, Michael is the descendent of an intellectual dynasty of sorts, the Grants, which includes some of the founding myth-makers of the liberal Anglo-Saxon establishment in Canada, as well as one of its most noteworthy dissidents, George Grant (Michael's uncle).

Michael, a first-born son, never seems to have doubted that he would someday inherit the exercise of political power himself. At the blue-blood-only Upper Canada College, a teenaged Ignatieff used to jaunt around campus with *Paris Match* under his arm and tell friends that one day he would be prime minister[1]. After a brief stint at age 18 campaigning for iconic Liberal leader Pierre Trudeau, he waited until late middle age to try to make good on his youthful boast. After more than 30 years abroad, Ignatieff returned to the country of his birth, and in 2008 became the leader of the opposition Liberal Party of Canada.

Most Canadian voters knew that their would-be prime minister had spent many years outside the country—the governing Conservative party ran a series of ads in 2009 to drive the point home—but many were not aware that the bulk of those years abroad were spent in the UK, first at Cambridge and then as a public commentator and intellectual, writing novels, screenplays and non-fiction while also hosting and producing television programs and documentaries. Long before his infamous backing of the Bush administration's foreign policy, Ignatieff similarly shocked and alienated many during the pitched class battles between the coal miners and the Thatcher government. This was the moment, Ignatieff says, when he realized for certain that he was a liberal, not a socialist, and it marked a rupture with some of his friends and colleagues.

During his time in the UK, Ignatieff grew close to Isaiah Berlin, considered by many the preeminent liberal thinker in the post–World War II era. A Russian-born Jew whose family, like Ignatieff's, had left after the 1917 Revolution, Berlin was an exile who nevertheless scaled the peaks of influence in both the UK and the United States. Ignatieff would become the older man's authorized biographer, and Berlin's ideas continue to inform both his own thinking and contemporary political debates. As it was for Berlin, whose advocacy of "negative liberty" stressed so-called "pluralism" over equality, radical social change is anathema to Ignatieff: "Since life is often a matter of choosing between evils rather than goods, I prefer the evils of capitalist individualism to the evils of collectivism" (RR, p. 23). The implications of Berlin's liberalism will be explored in what follows, in particular as they apply to Ignatieff's failed effort to rescue Canada's Liberal Party in a period of economic crisis.

Ignatieff spent much of the 1990s advocating for western military intervention in the Balkans. His prolific publishing record in this decade included a series of books on the wars that led to the break up of Yugoslavia. One of them, *Blood and Belonging*, which looked at the question of nationalism more generally, grew out of a television series he had made for the BBC. Before the turn of the millennium, Ignatieff had put himself at the center of debates about war and peace in the post–Cold War era.

As a champion of NATO and—increasingly—of the application of US military power generally, it was perhaps natural that Ignatieff should have skipped back across the pond in 2000 to accept a prestigious post at the Carr Center for Human Rights at Harvard. A stolen election and an act of mass murder on September 11, 2001 combined to precipitate the War-on-Terror/Axis-of-Evil years, and Ignatieff wasted little time jumping in with both feet. He soon emerged as one of the most important propagandists for war in the Bush era; what's more, he even started to self-identify, on occasion, as an American. Abandoning the urbane anti-theism he used to showcase in the pages of the *London Review of Books*, he now invoked not just Evil but, from time to time in his columns, God himself.

Every historical epoch calls forth its own intellectuals, both courtiers and critics. With the end of the Cold War, both types of public thinker had to retool and recalibrate their arguments. Ignatieff had spent the 1990s tinkering with and testing out new arguments for US and NATO military aggression. By the time 9/11, Afghanistan, Iraq and the Patriot Act came around, Ignatieff was ready, willing, and able to lend his name, prestige, and liberal phraseology to the new imperial project, which he duly christened "Empire Lite." In the crucible of the months leading up to the "Shock and Awe" invasion of Baghdad in March 2003, Ignatieff was the toast of the pro-war town. Writing in some of the most influential publications in the English-speaking world, he announced to anyone who would listen: "The American Empire? Get used to it."

But the heavenly days at Harvard soon turned hellish for Ignatieff. After the scale of the debacle in Iraq became clear, his intellectual stock plummeted in D.C. A close colleague in the human rights community pilloried him as "probably the most important figure to fall into this category of hand-wringing, apologetic apologists for human rights abuses."[2] In part this was because before his August 2007 article in the *New York Times Magazine* admitting he was wrong on Iraq, Ignatieff had already aired his doubts about the war in voluminous, self-contradictory articles. The future now belonged to the likes of Fareed Zakaria, Samantha Power, and others who shared Ignatieff's fundamental belief in and commitment to US domination, but who had not so prominently championed Bush's war crimes. Within months of the invasion of Iraq, Ignatieff had become a diminishing asset in terms of his utility to the empire. For the American hegemon, he had been a very "useful idiot" indeed.[3]

Not that the gatekeepers of power didn't still show their gratitude from time to time. In its December 2009 issue, *Foreign Policy* magazine published its "Top 100 Global Thinkers" of the year. Michael Ignatieff was number 64 on the prestigious list:

Poised to become Canadian prime minister next year, only five years after leaving Harvard University's Carr Center for Human Rights Policy, Ignatieff is out to prove the relevance of academia—and big ideas—in politics. Ignatieff's writing on the sometime necessity of "violence ... coercion, secrecy, deception, even

violation of rights" to fight terrorism has made him a singular
voice among Canadian liberals.

While *FP* may have been generously optimistic about his political prospects, they were perhaps too honest by half regarding his
singularity among "Canadian liberals," given that the positions he
had taken in the "war on terror" were so blatantly out of step with
the sensibilities of the political center and left in Canada.

Ignatieff came under fire not just for his pro-war views but also
for his arguments concerning civil liberties and the war on terror.
His theoretical musings about the "violation of rights" took on a
nightmarishly concrete new meaning in 2004, as the profoundly
non-abstract images of the Iraq War emerged in photos from the
dungeons of Abu Ghraib. The revelations of torture coincided with
the publication of Ignatieff's book *The Lesser Evil*, whose own tor-
tured logic provided, in the words of one former colleague, the
"intellectual tools" to Donald Rumsfeld and a US administration
determined to act outside of international law and the laws of war.
The same ex-colleague even included Ignatieff among "torture's
new best friends." Ignatieff was furious and indignant at the charge,
but he didn't stick around long enough to carry on the debate. In
2004, mandarins from the then-governing Liberal Party in Canada
came calling with an offer Ignatieff could not refuse. In 2005, he
announced that he had taken a post at the University of Toronto.
Soon after, his political intentions in Canada were made clear.

In the 2006 Canadian federal election, Ignatieff easily won
a "safe" Liberal seat in Ontario, though many in his party fared
much worse, with the Conservatives winning a minority government. After the resignation of former Liberal Prime Minister Paul
Martin, Ignatieff immediately set about running for the party
leadership, narrowly losing in his bid later that year to the long-
shot candidate, Stéphane Dion. Nevertheless Ignatieff, much more
so than any of the other failed candidates, never took his eyes off
the leadership prize, and differed with Dion on a number of key
issues—sometimes publicly, but more often only behind closed

doors—such as the war in Afghanistan and Dion's much maligned "Green Shift" carbon tax policy. After a short-lived attempt at a coalition with Canada's social democratic party, the New Democrats (NDP), Dion was removed, and another leadership race preempted when two potential rivals bowed out in order to clear the path for Ignatieff's coronation. As party leader, he never lived up to the hype. From the beginning—and to the chagrin of the Liberal Party—monikers like "the new Pierre Trudeau" or even "Canada's Obama" miserably failed to stick.

Ignatieff's rapid political rise and fall raises a number of questions. What does it say about our world—especially the politics of the English-speaking western countries—that a person with his record can still pass as a "progressive," "center-left" politician? Moreover, what does this say about the Left, or at least the mainstream, parliamentary Left, such as it is? Canada's NDP have benefited from Ignatieff's political failure, but have proven themselves curiously unable—at times, seemingly unwilling—to stake out a clear, distinctive progressive politics in contrast to those of Ignatieff, who if anything has moved his party further to the Right. Most damning of all, the NDP went largely mute on the unpopular war in Afghanistan, right at the moment where its Liberal opponents had the most pro-war leader in living memory.

In an era of virtual politics and ever-shrinking attention spans, Ignatieff and his backroom boys now engaged in a war of position against his own prolific arguments for war and empire, and his infamous flirtations with torture. With the world suffering from neo-liberalism's "hangover" in the form of economic recession and crisis, and adjusting to a post-Bush, post-"war on terror" age, Ignatieff attempted to rebrand himself within the mainstream liberal tradition in his bid for power. But he not only lost the battle for the hearts, minds, and votes of Canadians—he ended up presiding over the most catastrophic electoral defeat in the history of the Liberal Party of Canada.

What remains to be determined is history's verdict among publics and intellectual communities on both sides of the

Atlantic. What is to be learned from Ignatieff's failed liberal interventions?

While working through my twenties as a member of what a dear friend labels the *lumpen petty-bourgeoisie*—paid work ranged from stints at meatpacking, box and potato chip factories, to a brief turn at teaching and finally to a number of independent media ventures—I imbibed from that great font of cosmopolitanism on the cheap, books. My reading, work experiences, family, friendships, and increasingly active participation in a wide variety of protest and community activities have made me the person I am today: a social justice activist, a leader in the anti-war movement, and a member of the political Left.

My political engagements are part of the reason I was motivated to produce this study of Ignatieff's writings and ideas. This book presents a radical critique of Ignatieff and of his version of liberalism. Informed by my own experiences in politics and my interpretation of world and Canadian history, I contend that a politics of parsing evils is less than the politics we require. Our globalized world is faced with staggering inequalities, a spiraling international cycle of war and terrorism, and an ecological crisis that portends mass extinction and threatens the very foundations of humanity's long-term survival on Earth.

Having worked on quixotic election campaigns for progressive candidates and as a writer and activist for social justice for more than a decade, I have seen first hand the role that the Liberal Party in particular plays in defusing radical critiques of Canadian society.

My participation in broad anti-war organizing—an all too rare recent example of the Left visibly articulating a majority position—was what first brought Michael Ignatieff to my attention. His arguments on foreign policy, carried in the weightiest publications, are precisely those I have challenged as part of an international movement against war and empire.

The zenith of our efforts came on February 15, 2003, when

simultaneous international protests against the Iraq War took place. All totaled, it was the largest global mobilization in world history, but in many ways this highpoint was quickly followed by the movement's nadir. I remember the shock, on the Saturday morning of the big rally in Vancouver, of seeing our local protest particulars announced on the front page of the city's main daily corporate newspaper. The square we had booked for our rally wasn't nearly big enough for the crowd. The experience was repeated in most of the major cities on the planet. In those heady days of globalized solidarity, we felt like we had built a powerful movement against war.

But then the invasion of Iraq went ahead anyway. The only Weapons of Mass Destruction (WMDs) ever found there belonged to the invading armies led by the US. In the years that followed, the destruction was massive: hundreds of thousands of Iraqis dead and millions more made refugees. Many of us, back in early 2003, knew intellectually that the anti-war movement was not really going to be able to stop the conflict. But the reality was nevertheless a shocking, awful, and demoralizing blow, and many activists dropped away.

For those of us who have stayed the course, there has been much work to do. In Canada, after 2003, our efforts soon refocused on Afghanistan, where our then prime minister, the Liberal Jean Chrétien, had dispatched an additional couple of thousand troops, in part as a sop to the Bush administration for not having sent troops to Iraq.

Fences were also mended between the big powers at the expense of the Haitian people: In 2004, Canada joined France and the United States in backing a coup which overthrew the elected government of Jean-Bertrand Aristide. This intervention was, for a time at least, justified by invoking the then nascent Responsibility to Protect Doctrine, which Ignatieff had a hand in developing. The Canada Haiti Action Network, among others, asked the right question, "Responsibility to protect whom?" Aristide had been previously overthrown in 1991, just months after winning an overwhelming democratic mandate to change his grossly stratified society. The reforms which the Haitian president had in mind were telegraphed by his modification of an old creole proverb, "*Woch nan dio pa konnen doule woch nan soley.*" The rock in the water does not know the pain of the rock in the sun. Aristide tweaked this: "The rocks in the water are going to find out how the rocks in the sun feel." But the world's biggest rocks were not willing to let this happen. Since 2004, a UN armed force has occupied Haiti, and Aristide was only allowed to return after seven years in exile during which his party had been systematically repressed and excluded from the political process.

It's worth making explicit that I do not intend this book to serve in any way as a partisan flyer. The NDP, the natural beneficiaries of a left-wing critique of Ignatieff's positions, will also come in for plenty of criticism. As ever, the question for the political Left is: What is to be done in the face of the present economic and ecological crises, irrespective of the hypocrisies of liberal and conservative political elites?

Inevitably some will charge that to engage in any thorough critique of Michael Ignatieff is "objectively" to side with Stephen Harper and the Conservatives in Canada. Prior to the last election, this was a typical Liberal Party line: "If you vote for the NDP, the Bloc, or the Greens to send Stephen Harper a message, you'll get Stephen Harper—and he won't get the message." This argument reflects a fatally narrow conception of politics, which is reduced to the choice a voter makes between party brands every few years. As in the United States, and in most hollowed-out western democracies, elections are taken as the whole point of politics, rather than as a reflection of the balance of forces at a given point in time. Parties have become exclusively electoral machines that have voters and donors, but hardly members and activists, let alone anything like a meaningful, engaged social base. This is an evil that must be transcended.

One of Ignatieff's favorite catchphrases back when he hosted "The Late Show" on the BBC was: "Let's broaden the frame."

We urgently need to broaden the frame in which politics is discussed. Whether through sheer alienation and apathy, or due to a more sophisticated rejection of conventional politics, electorates all across the western world are tuning out. The economic crisis that began in 2008 has mobilized some renewed participation, but for the most part the Right has benefited more than the Left. For progressive-minded people to succeed in turning this reality around, we are going to have to construct a new politics, one bold enough both to challenge the stubborn vestiges of neo-liberal dogma and to offer a transformative vision beyond the logic of capitalism itself.

A common view of Michael Ignatieff's life and voluminous writings is that his is the story of an ambitious and accomplished progressive intellectual—the very definition of the "Renaissance Man" of ideas and action—who briefly championed misguided neo-conservative policies during the disorienting post-9/11 years. Chastened, he returned home to assume his political destiny while offering a mea culpa for his support of the war on Iraq. On this reading, Ignatieff, though he strayed, is still viewed as contributing to a progressive, enlightened political tradition that values human rights and diversity.

But a more radical interpretation of Ignatieff's intellectual and political trajectory is required—especially in these crisis-ridden times when the old dogmas of neo-liberalism have lost their unchallenged legitimacy. As with his hero and biography subject, Isaiah Berlin, Ignatieff's championing of human rights has always masked his identification with political and economic elites, his class arrogance, and his preference for violent control of "frontier zones" and suppression of the "barbarians" on the margins of empire.

In fact, from the pitched battles between Thatcher and the coal miners in the 1980s—one of the opening salvos in neo-liberalism's 30-year offensive—to the Balkan wars of the 1990s, to Iraq, Afghanistan, and right up to Israel's 22-day slaughter in Gaza in early 2009—Ignatieff and his political tradition have stood in opposition to fundamental human rights, the extension of democracy, and the pursuit of economic equality.

If this is indeed the Lesser Evil, then it is surely not good enough.

# 1 THE SOLIPSISTIC COSMOPOLITAN

*A country begins to die when people think life is elsewhere and begin to leave.*—Michael Ignatieff, *True Patriot Love*

*Born on third, thinks he got a triple*—Pearl Jam, "Bushleaguer"

Al Capone, notorious underworld boss of America's "second city," famously shrugged off North America's "second country" with pithy indifference: "I don't even know what street Canada is on." In the years since, unfortunately, the True North has earned similar contempt from ostensibly more enlightened sources. British historian Eric Hobsbawm once dismissed Canada as "culturally provincial, though interesting things and people occasionally emerge from it"[1]. Ken Kesey, the late American author of *One Flew Over the Cuckoo's Nest*, expressed a similar lack of interest in all things Canadian. An icon of the counter-culture and self-described link between the Beatniks and the hippies, Kesey's open mind couldn't take in the giant country just to his north. He assessed the prospects for the advent of the "New Consciousness": "Europe was too stiff to bring it off, Africa too primitive, China too poor. And the Russians thought they had already accomplished it. But Canada? Canada had never even been considered."[2]

Although they were not in search of the new consciousness, the Ignatieff household of the 1960s appears to have shared a similar mental map. In his 2009 book *True Patriot Love: Four Generations in Search of Canada*, a literary project admittedly dusted off to bolster his Canadian *bona fides*, Ignatieff recalls a little ditty his mother used to sing around the house in the sleepy capital city of Ottawa.

> I grew up in a Canadian household where my parents did think that life was elsewhere. This is how it is in small countries and provincial societies everywhere in the world. My mother used to go around the house humming a Judy Garland song with a line about how, if you haven't played the Palace, you might as well be dead. The Palace Theatre was elsewhere—not in Ottawa, where I grew up, but in the big bright world beyond. So the family question wormed its way into how I thought of my life, and the answer I gave myself was to get out of here, to go out into the bright world beyond and play the palace. (TPL, p. 28)

The real testing ground of his life lay elsewhere. So off he went. It would appear that in the young Michael's mind a precocious certainty emerged that he would be one of those rare noteworthies to come *from* Canada, and that meant hightailing it out of his mediocre homeland. He reports back proudly, "I played the palace in London for twenty years, as a journalist and writer, and for five years at Harvard as a professor."

This confession in the opening pages of *True Patriot Love* would seem to be an effort to tackle head-on the obvious tension between Ignatieff's wandering CV—over 30 years outside of Canada—and his newly asserted political aspirations in his homeland. For much of his adult life, Ignatieff led a highly self-conscious "cosmopolitan" existence, going so far as to deny the need for a home country at all. He seemed to take pleasure in "re-inventing" himself and "making it up as he [went] along," from affecting the speech of the British to adopting the militarist zeal of American neoconservatives. Nevertheless, returning to Canada as he approached his 60th birthday, Ignatieff became a born-again patriot. The wide-ranging circle of his life would prove difficult to square with the requirements of Canadian electoral politics. Even given the usually forgiving, soft-nationalist, and often insecure Canadian psyche, it would prove difficult for Ignatieff to overcome the impression that he was a Nowhere Man—the quintessential carpetbagger opportunist.

As the son of a diplomat, it's not surprising that he has led an itinerant life. Weeks after Michael Ignatieff was born on May 12, 1947, his father George—a powerful mandarin in the postwar Canadian bureaucracy—moved the family to New York, following his appointment as ambassador to the United Nations.

Michael's early years in New York were just the beginning of a dizzyingly globetrotting life. In his voluminous autobiographical writings, his introductory preamble inevitably references his "cosmopolitan" credentials. "If anyone has a claim to being a cosmopolitan, it must be me," he writes in the introduction to *Blood and Belonging*. A true blue blood, Ignatieff belongs to a privileged, ruling class clan on both his mother's and his father's side. His father's people were the aristocratic elite of the bygone Russian Empire. It's not hard to envisage Michael's czarist background, given his patrician bearing, sharp physical features, severe and even pained facial expressions. His bushy eyebrows are a caricaturist's dream (at one point, during an interview with a comedian on the French-language station Radio-Canada, Ignatieff was put in the unenviable position of addressing the embarrassing fact that a Facebook page devoted to his eyebrows had more fans than his own, official, page; this was then followed by a surreal exchange about the problem of his eyebrows being too social-democratic: "I need liberal eyebrows, at least"[3]). Grandfather Paul Ignatieff was the last Minister of Education in czarist Russia. Narrowly escaping execution at the hands of the Bolshevik Revolution, he initially took his family to the UK, before settling for exile in Canada. Great-grandfather Nicholas Ignatieff is an infamous figure in Russian history. As a ruthless diplomat, he defended Russia's imperial claims against her British, Ottoman, and Austro-Hungarian rivals; Nicholas took part in drawing the national boundaries in the Balkans, the twentieth century's ultimate powder keg. As Minister of the Interior in the early 1880s, he presided over the worst anti-Jewish pogroms of the nineteenth century.

In *The Russian Album* (1987), Ignatieff set out to examine the history of his Russian ancestors whom he "chose" because they were more "exotic," and since he could "always count on my mother's inheritance" (RA, p. 10). In concluding this exploration of his czarist forebears young Michael's synthesis dwells primarily on his own journey, seemingly disavowing the Russian roots he has just examined:

> I do not believe in roots ... I am an expatriate Canadian writer who married an Englishwoman and makes his home overlooking some plane trees in a park in north London. That is my story and I make it up as I go along. Too much time and chance stand between their story and mine for me to believe that I am rooted in the Russian past. Nor do I wish to be. I want to be able to uproot myself when I get stuck, to start all over again when it seems I must. I want to live by my wits rather than on my past. I live ironically, suspicious of what counts as self-knowledge, wary of any belonging I have not chosen. (RA, p. 185)

In both its style and choice of subject matter, his work suggest a restless, intense self-focus. A close reader of Ignatieff once noted that "personal pronouns litter his work."[4] Indeed, a number of his books begin with lengthy meditations about his reasons for writing. In *True Patriot Love*, he unguardedly concedes: "I can see how vain and distorted our family myth making could be, but for all that, I cannot disavow it. It is part of me" (TPL, p. 23). Ironically, it was to a family retreat in France that Ignatieff escaped to finish writing *True Patriot Love*, within weeks of taking over as Liberal Party leader in late 2008.

For his *Blood and Belonging* journeys—shot as a documentary series for the BBC and then put down in book form—Ignatieff admits: "I chose places I had lived in, cared about, and knew enough about to believe that they could illustrate certain central themes" (BB, p. 14). Ignatieff has published three novels, each of which touches on material from his own life. The most critically acclaimed of these, *Scar Tissue*, is a description of a family with two sons living through their mother's painful decline through Alzheimer's disease. Ignatieff is also nearly always a central character in his non-fiction books—at least he won't have to spend his last years scrambling to put his memoirs together. One might argue that Ignatieff's declarative, autobiographical style is more honest than the faux detachment of much non-fiction writing. I would argue that his style suits both his purposes and his times. His writings on issues of war and peace, in particular, are light on history and politics. When they are invoked, it is often in passing, and rarely in detail.

In their place, we get psychological explanations and plain moralizing. The latter is buttressed by an attitude of *j'y étais, donc je sais*;[5] Ignatieff's arguments often cite his personal experience. But paraphrased anecdotes are no substitute for historically informed analysis, and on closer inspection the fact of Ignatieff's having "been there" is usually beside the point. Anyway, he was no Robert Fisk.[6] Even as a war reporter he was really a war commentator, most often arriving after the main fighting to pontificate and lay blame.

A solipsistic style is one thing, but more important are the political consequences of this kind of focus on one's own reflection. All politicians and leaders in their fields will tend to have a high opinion of their own abilities. Canadian columnist Rick Salutin, however, observed that something more disconcerting is at play with Ignatieff, dubbing him "Narcissieff":

My own sense is that he'll make a seriously bad candidate, due to what I'd call his narcissism. This isn't so much about adoring yourself, as being so self-absorbed that your sense of how others react to you goes missing. A therapist I know says it usually involves "a great deal of self-referencing. A real other doesn't exist except as an extension of themselves." This won't be useful when you're asking for people's votes, against other candidates.[7]

Ignatieff's repeatedly asserted cosmopolitanism seemed intertwined with his introspective writing, and his apparent need and desire to carve his own path, to "uproot" himself, and to "start all over again." In a recent work, radical US-based geographer David Harvey draws attention to salient critiques of the faddish re-emergence of so-called cosmopolitanism in certain quarters:

> The optimistic cosmopolitanism that became so fashionable following the Cold War, Craig Calhoun points out, not only bore all the marks of its history as "a project of empires, of long-distance trade, and of cities," it also shaped up as an elite project reflecting "the class consciousness of frequent travelers." As such, it more and more appeared as "the latest effort to revive liberalism" in an era of neo-liberal capitalism. It is all too easy, concurs Saskia Sassen, "to equate the globalism of the transnational professional and executive class with cosmopolitanism."[8]

Indeed, Ignatieff's cosmopolitan travels and intellectual journey chart the trajectory of liberalism during the years of neo-liberal capitalism's heyday. He lived in neo-liberalism's ideological and military centers—Margaret Thatcher's Britain in the 1980s, George W. Bush's United States in the first years of the twenty-first century. In the realm of ideas, he traveled from the consensus left liberalism (sprinkled with Marxian analysis) of the social sciences in the academy of the 1970s and early '80s all the way to leading ideological sorties for the neo-conservative pack as they played out their violent, transformative fantasies with the might of the US empire. His political trajectory was not one of a Left apostate like Christopher Hitchens; it is, rather, a liberal reflection of the political retreats of the Left over the past three decades or more of neo-liberal dominance.

Ignatieff's around-the-world adventures began with his child-hood years in the Big Apple, followed by stints in Belgrade, Paris, Toronto, and Ottawa. He was then dispatched to the male finishing school of choice for Canada's blue bloods, Ontario's Upper Canada College. This was followed by an adult itinerary which included Vancouver, Paris, London, Berlin, and journeys to Russia, the Ukraine, Yugoslavia, Rwanda, the Congo, Afghanistan, Iraq, Haiti, and more. This doesn't include vacations, for which the family villa in the South of France has served many times for reunions and retreats, both romantic and literary.

## UPPER CANADA COLLEGE: PREP SCHOOL FOR PRIGS

Modeled on Eton College in England, Upper Canada College is Canada's oldest and most prestigious elite prep school; Prince Phillip, for instance, remains on the Board of Governors. It was founded in 1829, and later moved to Deer Park, now an upper middle-class residential area. A good portion of the Canadian establishment has attended UCC,[9] including the media baron and convicted fraudster Conrad Black, who has always worn his expulsion from the College as a badge of honor.

In the early 1960s, when 11-year-old Michael arrived, the College remained a stronghold of Tory conservatism. In a penetrating *Globe and Mail* piece on Ignatieff, Michael Valpy notes that his years at UCC were an unqualified success:

> When he graduated in 1965, he was steward—prefect—of his board-ers' house, captain of the first soccer team, academically at the top of his class, president of the debating club, editor of The College Times yearbook, a member of the library and chapel committees, chair of UCC's United Appeal, winner of the school's Nesbitt Cup for debating and a sergeant in the college cadet corps.[10]

By his own account, the prep school is also where "[he] learned to be an authoritarian prig." One episode with his younger brother Andrew, which Valpy cites, is especially irksome.

Andrew followed him to UCC in 1962. A self-described "fat little prick," he was absent his brother's talents. He was not an athlete, not adept at writing and public speaking, not competitive. While Michael was "God," and "everybody bowed and scraped when he passed," Andrew became known as "fatty," "piggy," "slob," "spaz," "big ass"—and "Iggy," a nickname he loathed.

Andrew, like Michael, contributed to *Old Boys*, a collection of reminiscences of UCC—it's the last public comment he has made about his brother:

Before I started at age 12, our parents sat down with my older brother and me. They said, "Michael, you're the big brother, and Andrew is going to UCC for the first time. It's the first time he has ever been away. You have to understand you have to be good to him."

Michael was very sweet and he told me how wonderful UCC would be. Then we went to my Aunt Helen's house and again he was very sweet. My Aunt Helen [Ignatieff, the boys' in loco parentis in Canada] again impressed on him the importance of him looking out for me. Then we went to the school and he introduced me to all the masters in the prep.

The next morning he said, "How are things going? Did you sleep well?" I said, "Yes, I slept well." He said, "How was the food?" I said, "It was gross." He said, "Do you want to go for a walk?"

We went for a walk, and he said, "I want to make one thing absolutely clear to you. When we're at Aunt Helen's house or Aunt Charity's house [Charity Grant, their mother's sister], you can say whatever you want to me. But if you ever see me on the school grounds, you're not to talk to me. You're not to recognize that I'm your brother. You don't exist as far as I'm concerned. Do I make myself clear?"

This moment of adolescent cruelty foreshadowed, in some ways, later incidents where Ignatieff seemed to sharply turn against friends and colleagues. It also exemplified that inability to really see, or at least to care about, how others reacted to him. In his UCC yearbook, Ignatieff tersely concluded his brief entry, "Intention: journalism or politics." He did not waste any time. He had barely begun his studies at the University of Toronto in 1965 when a federal election was called, and so Ignatieff threw himself into the unsuccessful campaign of Liberal Marvin Gelber, a friend of his parents. The next summer he worked at the *Globe and Mail* as an intern. With the onset of the political and cultural upheaval of the times, Ignatieff dabbled in anti-war activity, organizing a teach-in at the university and even participating in a sit-in against recruiting by Dow Chemical, the supplier of the napalm and Agent Orange that were decimating the people and landscape of Southeast Asia.

His brief foray into the peace movement was encouraged by a new friend, Bob Rae. A Young New Democrat, Rae sparred politically and intellectually with Ignatieff. Despite the early partisan rivalry, their politics were in fact not far apart. Ignatieff and Rae became fast friends, and were roommates for a time. Rae would go on to be a conservative social democrat, fond of invoking Edmund Burke. As NDP premier of Ontario in the early 1990s, his austerity measures enraged the trade unions and alienated a generation of social democrat voters. Four decades after they first met, Ignatieff and Rae twice competed for the Liberal Party leadership. But while Rae remained in Canada and made the now familiar political evolution from provincial NDP leader to federal Liberal politician, Ignatieff had other plans. Soon after "carrying Pierre Trudeau's bags" on the 1968 Liberal leader's election campaign—a badge of honor waved around endlessly 40 years later—Ignatieff packed his bags, full of ambition, and headed for the UK.

For his graduate studies, Ignatieff went to Oxford, and later completed a Ph.D at Harvard.[11] During a London summer in the mid-1970s, he met his British first wife, Susan Barrowclough. Together they moved to Vancouver, British Columbia, setting up house in Point Grey. He taught Canadian history at the University of British Columbia, but after only two years he accepted a teaching position back in England, at Cambridge. In 1984 he left the academy for a career as a public intellectual, quickly becoming a ubiquitous presence in the British media. He wrote essays, books, and screenplays, produced documentaries and hosted television talk shows. GQ magazine dubbed him the "Bionic Liberal." After over 20 years in Britain, and following a difficult divorce from Barrowclough, Ignatieff decided it was time to start all over again.

The United States was an inevitable destination for Ignatieff-the-cosmopolitan in those brief, heady years following "the end of history," joyously announced by the fall of the Soviet bloc. Ignatieff had spent the 1990s chronicling the US-led interventions in the Balkans; now he would move right into the belly of the empire—and just in time. In 2000, Ignatieff accepted a teaching position at Harvard, as director of the Carr Center for Human Rights.

It was from his leafy perch in Cambridge, Massachusetts, that Ignatieff would launch his prolific arguments in support of the Bush administration's war on terror. In his drive for war, solipsism trumped prudent judgment. On the night that the "shock and awe" invasion of Iraq began, March 19, 2003, Ignatieff was out to dinner at Casablanca's with his Cambridge neighbor, Kanan Makiya, an ex-Trotskyist academic version of the scam artist Ahmed Chalabi, peddling delusions of the US being greeted in Baghdad as liberators to eager neo-conservative buyers in the White House and Pentagon. Makiya was reportedly the exile Dick Cheney cited for his infamous prediction that US forces in Iraq would be greeted "with sweets and flowers." Ignatieff would repeatedly make reference to his faith in "Iraqi exiles" or refer to an "Iraqi exile friend," when explaining how he could have erred so badly in helping lead the intellectual charge to war in Iraq. He could not see past his own Cambridge friend, and the powerful interests behind Makiya. He failed entirely to appraise realistically how the other—in this case millions of Iraqis with their own unique geographic and social conditions—might react to the foreign military occupation.

In January 2005, as evidence of the Iraq debacle accumulated, three "kingmakers" arrived in Cambridge from Toronto, Ontario. Ron Graham, a Liberal insider, tells the story in a furious essay in *The Walrus*, a Canadian magazine. Alf Apps, Ian Davey, and Dan Brock were powerbrokers in the Liberal Party of Canada, and they came calling on Ignatieff at Harvard to ask him to return to the country of his birth. Over dinner at the Charles Hotel, they made their pitch.

> Ignatieff would deliver a barnburner speech at the Liberal convention in March, move back to Canada by the fall, secure a perch at the University of Toronto, write a book, make a TV documentary, find a riding, knock on doors, and get elected. Though a rookie MP, he would ascend swiftly into the cabinet to sit at the right hand of Paul Martin, learn the ropes of Parliament and government for a couple of years, run for the leadership when Martin retired, win, and become prime minister of Canada.

Ignatieff bought it. As Graham imagines it, he bought it eagerly.

> What more appropriate destiny for the grandson of Count Pavel Ignatiev, minister of education to Czar Nicholas II, and the scion of a prominent clan of British imperialists, Upper Canadian academics, and distinguished diplomats? Hadn't young Michael proclaimed it his intention as a lad on the playing fields of Upper Canada College? By the end of the meal, according to one participant, the question wasn't "why?" but "how?"
>
> It wasn't unlike the urban legend, often attributed to Margaret Atwood, of the brain surgeon who tells her at a dinner party that he's thinking of writing a novel after he retires. "Oh, that's a coincidence," she is supposed to have said. "I'm thinking of becoming a brain surgeon."[12]

As Makiya proved with Iraq, an exile's dream of triumphant return can tend to blur reality. If the title were not already taken, the story of Michael Ignatieff's return to Canada could be published as "Beyond Chutzpah." Friends and close associates insisted that

Ignatieff kept in close touch with his home country during his 30-plus years of self-imposed exile. However, as was so often the case, his own words stood as an indictment. In 2000, Ignatieff was invited back to Canada to give the prestigious Massey Lectures, hosted by the Canadian Broadcasting Corporation (CBC). A preparatory retreat in the luxurious Rocky Mountain resort town of Banff helped Ignatieff to catch up on developments in his home country. His lectures, published as *The Rights Revolution*, set out his views on Canadian human rights developments in the decades he was out of the country. In the introduction to the published version of *The Rights Revolution* he picked an out-of-this-world metaphor to illustrate the effect of his having lived abroad for decades: "I want to alert readers that I am a Martian outsider." Strangely, Ignatieff omitted his years teaching Canadian history in Vancouver, noting: "I am writing about the rights talk of a country of which I am a citizen, but in which I have not resided since 1969. In some sense these lectures are my attempt to catch up with the turbulent history of my country in the very years I was abroad." He even implied that he was—happily—a man without a country. Canada, he said, was "the place on earth that, if I needed one, I would call home" (RR, pp. x–xi).

Political scientist Stephen Clarkson seemed to imply that only extreme self-regard could have spurred Ignatieff's late mid-life quest for political power in Canada: "[He] has no political experience, didn't know the party's program and the staff. He had everything to learn, except for where Canada is on a map ... Politics is a very difficult thing to learn at 60."[13]

Having so recently disavowed his need for Canada, it should have been obvious that it was going to be a tough sell convincing people to let him run. Even the most high-functioning workaholic would clearly struggle to reacquaint him or herself with the particular political, social, economic, and cultural context.

But once again, Ignatieff allowed himself to be deluded by courtiers in Cambridge, and thus embarked on his last invasion. Canadians did not greet him with flowers or sweets, nor with good polling numbers. In one of the most recent surveys, assessing the popularity of the country's federal political leaders, Ignatieff's rival to the right, Stephen Harper, was awarded a "C+"; to his left, Jack Layton got an "A." Unfortunately for the Liberals, Canadians couldn't spell Ignatieff without an "F."[14] His leadership has led the Liberals into a quagmire that ended with their Conservative rivals enjoying a majority government (given the fall-out from military adventurism in the Balkans and the Middle East, this is arguably not the first time that religious fundamentalist and conservative elements have indirectly benefited from one of Ignatieff's missteps). As opposition leader, Ignatieff never inspired confidence, even in his own ranks, and only the fear of chaos and open civil war among the Liberals prevented his being ditched as leader prior to an election. The morning after Ignatieff's humiliating election defeat on May 2, 2011, he ignominiously withdrew from Canadian politics.

Ever the reporter-diarist, Ignatieff sometimes spoke as if he was a journalist observing his own political travails. In late 2010, he told a Canadian reporter that he'd been keeping notes about his Canadian adventure. "One day I'll get back and write some of this stuff up."[15] It's not clear what Ignatieff meant by "get back"—to England? To Harvard? He certainly couldn't have meant getting back to a relentless focus on his own story—that's a preoccupation he's never left.

# 2 THE NEGATIVES OF LIBERALISM

With the publication of *A Just Measure of Pain*, Michael Ignatieff quickly developed a reputation as a serious young progressive intellectual. His interests and standing brought him into contact with a group of like-minded academics organized around the *History Workshop Journal*, whose animating spirit and founder was Raphael Samuel. In 1981, Ignatieff contributed an essay on "Marxism and Classical Political Economy" to a collection edited by Samuel, *People's History and Socialist Theory*.

Barbara Taylor, co-director of the Raphael Samuel History Centre, has written an accessible overview of Samuel's life and the journal that he helped found,[1] She explains that Samuel was a life-long socialist, whose work was informed by the motto "History is too important to be left just to professional historians." The journal grew out of a series of popular education workshops designed to teach "history from below." While not bound by rigid sectarian-ism, the publication was "clearly informed by Marxian analysis," even issuing a manifesto with its launch issue:

> Our journal will be dedicated to making history a more demo-cratic activity—and a more urgent concern—by reaffirming the unity of teaching and scholarship, learning and life. We believe that history is a source of inspiration, a means of understanding the present and the best critical vantage point from which to view the present.[2]

In addition to writing for and helping to edit the budding journal, Ignatieff co-edited with Istvan Hont a collection of scholarly articles, *Wealth and Virtue: The Shaping of Political Economy in the Scottish Enlightenment*. Their introductory essay is a sophisticated consideration of Adam's Smith legacy, arguing "that the Wealth of Nations was centrally concerned with the issue of justice, with finding a market mechanism capable of reconciling inequality of property with adequate provision for the excluded."[3]

Ignatieff also published a regular column in the left-liberal *New Statesman* and later the *Observer*. He earned praise as a versatile writer. Together with friend Hugh Brody, he explored his interest in Freudian psychoanalysis by writing a screenplay, *Nineteen Nineteen*. For the book version, John Berger contributed an Afterword, praising the work for speaking "directly to what we know about life, composed inextricably of the most intimate movements of the heart, accident, and remorseless movement of history."

The major historical movements in the Britain of the 1980s were driven ahead by a remorseless Conservative government bent on breaking the power of the organized working class. The titanic battles between the government of Margaret Thatcher and the coal miners would come to define a decade of attacks against unions and the Left. In 1984, it was still the early years of neo-liberalism's ascendancy, but a clear pattern was emerging—Thatcher's Britain and the United States under Ronald Reagan were in the vanguard of this capitalist fightback.

For Ignatieff, the miners' strike was a pivotal moment that would uproot him from his circle of friends and colleagues, and help to define his thinking as hostile to the Left. Contrary to the portrayal of Ignatieff as a consistent left-liberal who only cast aside his progressive beliefs in defense of Bush's war in Iraq, the truth is that the rot set in much earlier. Or perhaps it was always there.

In December 1984, Ignatieff wrote a long piece for *New Statesman* about "the agonies of the miners' strike." On the cover of the magazine is a socialist-realist(ish) drawing of a policeman pushing back against lines of striking miners on the march. Also depicted are proud Labour women carrying banners emblazoned with the question, "Which Side Are We On?" Early on in Ignatieff's article, it is in fact difficult to tell which side he's on. Only upon closer examination does it become clear that he is not on the side of the miners. The essay was one of Ignatieff's signature acts of uprooting or starting again—and in the process cutting ties with his progressive former friends. The tone and style of the piece is familiar, already the author's mature voice. Characteristically, he lets his argument shift from side to side, making it clear that he understands all the different positions, and throwing out plenty of caveats.

Regretting the "virulent and abusive language on both sides of the disputes," Ignatieff laments the fact that a compromise—which he viewed as reasonable, realistic, and attainable—seemed unlikely to be reached. He criticizes Thatcher for putting "law and order" into "the void in Conservative rhetoric where an idea of the common good ought to be." He deplores the "political strategy explicitly seeking to smash the NUM [National Union of Miners]," and warns that such a scorched-earth policy will leave a "legacy of bitterness." Most of Ignatieff's admonishments, however, are reserved for the miners and their supporters on the Left:

> The fact that it is the State, not Capital, which is against the miners also transforms the casus belli—the definition of the uneconomic pit   into an issue about the social allocation of common resources. If the mines were in private hands, the argument that there are no economic grounds for closure might have sounded like a dignified socialist refusal to allow the law of profit to dictate the future of working people's communities ...

And so on. Ignatieff asserts that this is a longstanding problem for the ideological Left in its support for public sector unions, claiming that "The public sector strikes of 1973–1979 destroyed the moral legitimacy of the union movement and prepared the electoral basis for Thatcherism within the working class itself." Ignatieff disagrees sharply with "those on the Left who maintain that the miners' strike is a vindication of a class-based politics." This was the moment in Ignatieff's life, he claims, when he realized definitively that he was a liberal and not a socialist. Oddly, he attributes this in part to his revulsion at the class nature of British society. Valpy recounts Ignatieff's version of this "aha!" moment of anti-socialist clarity, which came to him at a fundraiser for the miners held in a middle-class North London home.

> He says he became acutely aware of how much he hated the British class system. He saw how wrong he had been to think that, as an expatriate Canadian, he had been handed a sort of free pass to stand apart from what he saw as class games being played by his left-wing friends.
>
> He realized that, despite the years he had spent with the History Workshop, he was not a socialist; he was a liberal—"left of centre, but always a liberal." He knew he was no Thatcherite, but he felt that Britain could not continue to produce so much coal and the left was being intellectually dishonest in not accepting the fact.[4]

Not for the last time Ignatieff was positioning himself as the progressive telling hard truths to a more ideological and unrealistic Left—in other words speaking truth to the powerless (or just simply speaking power). Perhaps in anticipation of the backlash he would face, Ignatieff closes his essay by predicting that history will absolve him, and will "not judge kindly" those in both camps "who welcome the dawn of an era of the politics of class versus the politics of the market."

Ignatieff's condescending prescriptions for the Left notwithstanding, the struggle between the working class and Thatcherism was unavoidable; indeed, this was a class struggle launched by the ruling class. Ignatieff wanted no part of it, but as the legendary late American historian Howard Zinn has famously pointed out, "you can't be neutral on a moving train"; even if that train is no longer running on coal power. Alienated from the History Workshop group, Ignatieff quickly began to move in different circles. Ditching the Left almost never hurts one's career prospects, but in reality he was already well on his way, having left his academic post to begin what would quickly become a successful career as a freelance commentator and writer. His first non-academic book, *The Needs of Strangers*, had been published earlier in the year.

Ignatieff's liberalism, denuded of those unseemly class politics, quite naturally brought him into regular contact with Isaiah Berlin, by then an aging Oxford don and one of the most renowned liberal, anti-communist western intellectuals of the post–World War II period. In the late 1980s, Ignatieff and Berlin began regular conversations about the older man's life and times. They eventually agreed on a project for an authorized biography, *Isaiah Berlin: A Life*. Berlin did not ask to vet anything, however; in fact, he stipulated that the biography was to be published posthumously.

Berlin is best known for his "Two Concepts of Liberty," originally delivered as a lecture at Oxford in 1958 and broadcast by the BBC. Berlin contrasted negative liberty and positive liberty; he claimed no great originality, and conceded that others had explored similar ideas about the tensions between positive and negative freedoms. Somewhat counter-intuitively, it was "negative liberty" which Berlin deemed the more positive of the two. By this he meant freedom from undue coercion, violence, and instruction by the state or other powerful actors bent on imposing a single way of being on free individuals; "positive liberty" was associated with the negatives of overly centralizing authorities and excessive enforced homogeneity, whether economic, political, or cultural. Against totalitarianism of all shades, from the undemocratic, forced collectivism of the communist states to the brutal, atavistic crimes of fascism, Berlin advocated a value-pluralism. For Berlin, the dangerous opposite of pluralism is monism—the philosophical position that "only one set of values is true, all the others are false." It was the creative application of Berlin's pluralism that produced Ignatieff's most useful contributions to Canadian public life, arguing against some of the most entrenched views of Canada's Anglophone majority. In *The Rights Revolution*, for instance, Ignatieff defends Quebec Law 101 privileging the French language in that province, and advocates greater aboriginal self-government. Unfortunately, Ignatieff the politician did not spend much time developing or expounding on similar progressive proposals.

As the saying goes, even a broken clock is right twice a day, and though Ignatieff was rarely correct in his assessment of just how much wisdom he had to impart to the Left, his relationship with Berlin, and engagement with the latter's political biography, was instructive. Though Ignatieff's multiple family histories and autobiographical writings betray a certain self-indulgence, with Berlin, the young liberal author took a strong and genuine interest in the ideas expounded by one of liberalism's standard-bearers. There is something to be said for taking seriously the ideas that have moved one's political forebears to action—for instance, whatever the shortcomings of progressive politics of all shades in the twentieth century (and they were legion), we should not give in to the temptation to discard all of the ideas, traditions, and sensibilities of the Left too quickly. Ignatieff deserves credit for—while still a young man—engaging deeply with the ideas of Berlin and others in his tradition. The Left needs to take the history of its own ideas and movements just as seriously, the better to immunize itself against the communications specialists, facilitators, marketing grads and PR flacks who genuinely believe that they know more than the organizers, activists, and workers.

Perhaps the most egregious form of identity politics to take root on the Left is the cult of youth. I cringe to think of how many times I played the "age card" to buttress an intervention at a political meeting: "If we really want to get young people involved we have to ..." Ostensibly a sincere appeal to take up the issues of most concern to the young, it's actually a sad reflection of the internalization of consumer capitalist society's inversion of the notion of the "wisdom of elders." In my experience, the Left too rarely takes care to document and celebrate the lives and ideas of its elders, let alone provide special consideration for their opinions. In short, I think it's a shame that more young left intellectuals aren't writing biographies about or seriously studying the ideas of their predecessors.

The recent history of the British Labour Party should be warning enough of the dangers lurking down the seductive path of "new, new, new." Beware the pimply pseudo-sage who tells you that "the terms Left and Right are so *passé*." The young press-release-writing professional sometimes seems possessed by a certainty that they know better precisely because they know next to nothing.

Of course, for Ignatieff, publishing the definitive biography of Berlin was not without its benefits. The 1998 publication met with strong reviews; the writing is eloquent and avoids hagiography. George (formerly Douglas) Fetherling, a noted Canadian author and critic, pointed me to an early passage in the book about Berlin, with which he felt Ignatieff identified. The quotation in question was a "preemptive strike" which Berlin offered whenever he was asked about his overarching agenda: "I am an intellectual taxi; people flag me down and give me destinations and off I go" (IB, p. 7). (Ignatieff's own intellectual journey would, ultimately, lead him into making much more serious preemptive strikes.) Discussing this remark, Ignatieff dismissed Berlin's self-criticism, arguing that there was an overall coherence and purpose to his work:

> ... this was wrong ... Many of his essays were demanded of him by chance and circumstances, but he accepted only the assignments that fitted his itinerary. There is no doubt that there was an itinerary and, when he had completed it, the result was a unique and coherent body of work. To use the distinction he made famous, the range of his work may make him seem like a fox, who knows many things; in reality, he was a hedgehog, who knew one big thing ... (IB, p. 7)

One big thing that the two men had in common was that their families were émigrés from the Russian Revolution. Isaiah was a young child in revolutionary St. Petersburg (Leningrad). His father was a successful merchant, and the family had a large home with servants. The Revolution of 1917 at first did not upset this comfortable situation, but that soon changed. Frightening harbingers of the loss of their privileges surrounded the Berlin family, and the young Isaiah sensed the anxiety. By the winter of 1918–19, the revolutionary regime's class warfare had reached the family home in Petersburg, and now "even Isaiah realized that something menacing had begun to happen."

The house committee in Angliisky Prospekt ordered everyone to vacate their extra rooms in order to conserve heat. Isaiah slept with his mother, while his father slept next door in his study-office. For the next two and a half years their life was reduced to the compass of these two rooms, in an atmosphere of searches, privation and fear that forced them to turn ever more in upon themselves (IB, p. 28).

Out for a walk with one of the family servants in the months just before the Bolshevik takeover, Isaiah witnessed a czarist cop being grabbed by a gang of unruly protesters and dragged away. The story, as Berlin told it throughout his life, always implied that this protector of his family's class was taken away and executed, or at least roughly treated. As Berlin recalled it, this was the moment where he developed a life-long aversion to violence.

But violence by whom? In a dissenting opinion on Ignatieff's biography, Christopher Hitchens (whose departure schedule from the Left was slightly out of synch with his fellow war-on-terror pundit-hawk) lambasted Berlin for his refusal to denounce the Vietnam War, and Ignatieff for his failure to write at any length about this episode in Berlin's life. Having held a diplomatic post in the United States during World War II, Berlin returned in an academic capacity during the Vietnam War. In Washington, D.C., as Hitchens notes, Berlin quickly became a regular in the company of a group of pro-war, anti-communist intellectuals. As

Hitchens rightly points out regarding Berlin's well-noted distaste for violence,

> It would have been more precise to say: only for certain sorts of physical violence and political experiment. Policemen are supposed to control crowds, not crowds policemen. Vietnam, for example, was not just an instance of horrific premeditated violence. It was a laboratory experiment run by technician-intellectuals and academic consultants, who furnished us with terms like "interdict," "relocate," "body count" and "strategic hamlet."[5]

It was Berlin's failure to denounce the violence of the world's most powerful state that brought down the charge of hypocrisy. As Hitchens puts it, "he was simultaneously pompous and dishonest in the face of a long moral crisis where his views and his connections could have made a difference." But Michael Ignatieff, an avowed devotee of "negative liberty," went much further than mere compliant silence. Building up through the Balkan wars of the 1990s, he would end up advocating the violent, coerced road to "liberty" espoused by the neo-conservatives. In this endeavor he would be joined by Hitchens and a host of other ex-Trotskyists as well as Left apostates from other backgrounds. Had Isaiah Berlin been around to witness the ascendance of the neo-cons, he might have argued that they were just consistent monists who had switched teams halfway through the game, transferring the class or nation benefiting from their all-encompassing vision for violent and purifying transformation.

After the collapse of the Berlin Wall and the communist bloc, the bedrock foundation of monist beliefs on both Left and Right caved in. New possibilities and priorities opened up for global capitalism. First and among the foremost of these was the need to project power eastward through NATO's military might. In the 1990s, the frontline of this project was Yugoslavia, a communist holdout whose disintegration would take longer and cost far more blood than most.

# 3 BALKAN WARRIOR

*It wasn't hatred that destroyed Yugoslavia, so much as fear. Fear of freedom. Fear of the past.*—Michael Ignatieff, *Blood and Belonging*

*Nobody likes empires, but there are some problems for which there are only imperial solutions.*—Michael Ignatieff, *Empire Lite*

Perhaps sometimes a fox is really just a chameleon, able to blend seamlessly into his surroundings and survive in diverse climates. As the world's political colors changed, so too did Ignatieff's pre-occupations. In the early 1990s, he produced a television series called *Blood and Belonging* which explored issues of nationalism, visiting hot spots in Europe and North America. This included episodes dealing with Quebec, Northern Ireland, a newly united Germany and the newly independent Ukraine, where his Russian ancestors had held an estate. And then there was Yugoslavia, the key to the project and the canvas on which Ignatieff would paint his evolving views on military intervention, war, and empire as the decade proceeded.

Setting out to engage in a cosmopolitan's critique of modern nationalism, he distinguished between a destructive "ethnic nationalism," and a more collegial "civic nationalism." Ignatieff was not yet a strident, open advocate of imperialism. But he did already seem to lament its apparent absence from the post–Cold War world (BB, p. 11).

Despite his anti-nationalism, there were wince-inducing moments in the series that showcased a lingering case of Great Russian chauvinism. Riding the train into Kiev, for instance, Ignatieff explained, "My problem with taking Ukrainian nationalism seriously is that I have roots in this country and they're Russian. My family always called the Ukrainians little Russians." In the written version, Ignatieff expounded on his apparent disregard for these former czarist subjects, claiming that the then nascent independent Ukrainian state

> conjures up images of embroidered peasant shirts, the nasal whine of ethnic instruments, phony cossacks in cloaks and boots, nasty anti-Semites … Clearing customs, I feel like declaring my basic prejudices on arrival. Isn't nationalism just an exercise in kitsch, in fervent emotional insincerity? Especially so in the Ukraine. It has been part of Russia for centuries. Ukrainians now have a state, but are they really a nation? Into this inauthentic void streams nationalist emotionalism, striving to convince them that there always was a Ukrainian nation; that it has been suppressed for centuries; that it has at last found freedom, and so on. The reality is different. (BB, pp. 106–7)

Let's put aside the irony of a descendant of Nicholas Ignatieff treating "nasty" anti-Semitism as a foreign disease. The comments deriding Ukrainian nationhood came back to bite Ignatieff-the-politician, in the "safe" seat the Liberal Party machine opened up for him in the west Toronto riding of Etobicoke. Soon enough, Ignatieff's problem became apparent: the district had a significant population of Ukrainian immigrants, and they were outraged by Ignatieff's appointment, especially coming as it did via a skirting of the regular nomination process in order to accommodate the "star candidate." Ignatieff said his words were taken out of context, and the controversy eventually died down, only to be revived when, in his first shuffling of personnel after taking the party leadership, he moved Ukrainian MP Borys Wrzesnewskyj to the backbenches of the opposition, out of his important position as Immigration Critic.

Ignatieff's aversion to peoples formerly under the Russian sphere of influence also occasionally bubbled to the surface during the *Blood and Belonging* segments shot in Yugoslavia. His visit there took place amidst the wreckage of the war of secession fought by Croatia against the government in Belgrade, with the deadly poison of ethnic chauvinism still latent. The episode's title, "The Road to Nowhere," is Ignatieff's rechristening of the "Highway of Brotherhood and Unity," and suggests that he may have concluded that this once functional, multi-ethnic country was beyond repair. Before offering his diagnosis of the troubles, Ignatieff recalls fondly his childhood years when his father was a diplomat, summering on a lake a few hundred meters from Marshall Tito's summer place. "We used to travel down here every summer, in a big black Buick with lots of chrome," he said, while driving down the once optimistically named highway.

Driving into the town of Vukovar on the Serbian side of the new border, Ignatieff steps out of his car, surveys the lingering war damage, and vents his spleen at the ruin of Yugoslavia.

> Nobody has taken responsibility for this. It's what makes you sick about nationalism, it's a vocabulary in which everybody shifts the blame for whatever atrocity ... This is the main square of what [sigh] used to be an extremely nice Austro-Hungarian town ... This used to be a European city... Now the Serbs want to rebuild it ... But I've got a better idea. Leave it ... as a monument to that great European tradition, ethnic nationalism.

Next, Ignatieff visited Belgrade. In the early hours of the morning he and his film crew went down to interview some locals lining up to take their money out of the bank—Serbia, already facing sanctions from the west, was suffering from hyper-inflation. He had "expected a lot of anti-Milošević feeling" but instead he found anger at the west and at him personally. As Ignatieff tried to interview people in the line-up, one angry man launched into a rant about the western media, "You only tell lies."

The final crowd-shot in the documentary captured a singer entertaining a sparse crowd in one of Belgrade's town squares. Signing off from Serbia, it was hard to tell whether Ignatieff's narration was scolding the locals, or merely lamenting their hapless fate:

> Nationalism is a politics of fantasy. It offers people a glorious escape from the real world, from the grim second-rate-ness of Balkan life. So draw in the circle, toss in your worthless bank note, and try to forget the pain … This is the end of the road for me, but in a sense the road never ends. It's going to be a long time before anyone travels the Highway of Brotherhood and Unity Again.

No one had called an Ignatieff a liar in the Balkans since his great grandfather Nicholas was known as the "father of lies," for his ruthless scheming and skullduggery in pursuit of Mother Russia's strategic goals in the region. The great-grandson would also end up doing legwork in the Balkans for the big powers, but that's not how he first conceived of his endeavor. The twentieth-century Ignatieff took pains to let his readers know that he was well aware that in the preceding century "ivory, gold and copper sent the imperial agents into the heart of darkness" (WH p. 4). In the introduction to *The Warrior's Honour* he claims there is no "narrative of imperial rivalry or ideological struggle that compels the zones of safety to make the zones of danger their business." All competing meta-narratives, whether religious or Marxist or otherwise had "dishonoured themselves by the slaughter committed in their name" (WH, p. 10).

Perhaps, as the 1990s unfolded, Ignatieff came to think of it as his mission to help construct a new, unblemished narrative. In this effort, he naturally recognized television as a powerful weapon that could be wielded to compel citizens in the secure west to action, making it "harder to sustain indifference or ignorance." Touching on Live Aid, and the growth of organizations like Médecins Sans Frontières, Ignatieff describes the rise of the new "mobilizers of money and commitment"—which as we now know would grow into the massively bloated Non Governmental Organization (NGO) sector. As neo-liberal austerity measures and so-called shock therapy ravaged the public sectors of Third and Second World countries throughout the 1990s, Ignatieff correctly identified this new sector as part of an ascendant "antipolitics" which refused to take sides on ideological questions. In assessing the new landscape of war and global politics in the 1990s and its dissemination through television, Ignatieff was fair-minded enough to note that although television claims to be impartial, "in practice it worships power" (in this sense it is more than a little bit like Ignatieff himself). Further, he even noted that the newsroom rule of thumb in the west still held that "one British, American or European life is worth—in news value—a hundred Asian or African lives." (Again, at least when it came to Iraq and Afghanistan, Ignatieff engaged in a similar arithmetic.)

Where Ignatieff fell short in *The Warrior's Honour* was in his superficial and psychological explanations for the violent disintegration of Yugoslavia, reaching back to a study of Freud's from 1917 entitled "The Taboo of Virginity" in which, Ignatieff observed, "it is precisely the minor differences in people who are otherwise alike that form the basis of feelings of strangeness and hostility between them" (WH, p. 41). Further channeling the Austrian, Ignatieff writes about the pernicious long-term impacts of Tito's "emasculation" of his political opposition, and asserts that Serbs retained a centuries-old paranoid delusion of persecution.

Ignatieff supplemented these explanations with denunciations of "Western failures to act," a theme which would be built upon. This sort of eclectic and rather uncommitted (and sometimes condescending) descriptive writing only gave way to a full-on advocacy of western intervention with NATO's war against

Serbia over the disputed territory of Kosovo. But this emphasis on western inaction obscures the much more numerous cases of harmful western actions against smaller, less powerful states in the Global South, whether through overt, direct intervention or by the equally sinister but more covert means of supporting regressive regimes or overthrowing progressive ones. It was certainly not a western failure to act that doomed Chileans, Argentineans or Indonesians—to take just three out of dozens of possible examples —to endure bloodbaths and long years of military rule.

If an element of ethnic strife was what was required, then at least the plight of East Timor—which suffered for decades under a brutal Indonesian occupation—should have garnered some of Ignatieff's attention. In 1999, the west again abandoned East Timor to massacres by Indonesian forces; after thousands were killed, a peacekeeping contingent made up primarily of Australian forces belatedly arrived. No US attack on the capital Jakarta took place—such an action never appears even to have occurred to Ignatieff and his ilk. Nevertheless, on the other side of the world, the entire military might of the NATO countries was brought to bear in defense of a similarly small, subjugated province, but where, compared to East Timor, human rights abuses were actually being carried out on a smaller scale.

The smallest of the provinces seeking independence from Yugoslavia, Kosovo was home to a Muslim Albanian majority which had long suffered systemic discrimination from both the central government in Belgrade and the Serbian minority in the province. By the late 1990s, the ethnically Albanian Kosovars had taken up arms, organizing the Kosovo Liberation Army (KLA). As demands for independence grew louder, the Serbian state's repression and the corresponding cycles of reprisal by the rebels grew more deadly. The west had long sought to oust the Serb chauvinist Milošević regime, and they seized the opportunity to turn up the heat. At negotiations held in Rambouillet, France, US negotiator Richard Holbrooke presented the Serb leader with an offer he couldn't accept. As Noam Chomsky explains, the so-called "peace agreement" Holbrooke put on the table "called for complete military occupation and political control of Kosovo by NATO, and effective NATO military occupation of the rest of Yugoslavia at NATO's will."[1] In March 1999, a full-scale NATO bombing was launched.

Tony Blair (who like Ignatieff had dabbled in the British Left as a young man) became British prime minister in 1997 and immediately emerged as a leading advocate of western military intervention (unlike Ignatieff, the hyper-ambitious Blair, consumed by a sense of his destiny early on, never wasted any time penning nuanced Marxian essays). As with Iraq in 2003, in 1999 it was the United States (then under President Bill Clinton) and Tony Blair's UK who led the west into an illegal war. Never approved by the UN Security Council, the 78-day bombing contributed to the exodus of close to one million people from Kosovo, and claimed hundreds of casualties. Among the targets hit by the smart, humanitarian US bombers were a convoy of refugees, the headquarters of Serbian television, and the Chinese Embassy in Belgrade.

The war in Kosovo saw the first high-profile deployment of Blair's sanctimonious moralizing of imperial aims. His arguments, albeit delivered with more theatrics and zeal, echoed Ignatieff's. In April 1999, while the Kosovo war still raged, Blair chose to make his most significant speech on foreign policy to date in Chicago, where he unveiled the "Doctrine of the International Community." This was a clear signal that the overriding objective of British foreign policy under Blair would be to secure and strengthen the Atlantic alliance with the United States. (After 9/11, Blair doubled-down on this alliance of empires in very different stages of decline.) Much as Ignatieff would, Blair forcefully called on the US to act more aggressively as the world's policeman.

In Chicago, after outlining the broad strokes of New Labour's domestic program, Blair enumerated transparently self-serving rules for determining whether a military intervention should proceed. He concluded by urging the United States to live up to its true imperial destiny: "never fall again for the doctrine of isolationism. The world cannot afford it. Stay a country, outward-looking, with the vision and imagination that is in your nature."[2] In his 1999 *Virtual War*, Ignatieff approvingly summarizes this new Blair Doctrine of war:

> First, are we sure of our case? Second, have we exhausted all diplomatic options? Third, are there military operations "we can sensibly and prudently undertake"? Fourth, are we prepared for the long-term? And finally, do we have national interests involved? If we could answer these questions in the affirmative, we should intervene. The Prime Minister believed the Kosovo intervention cleared these hurdles. (VW, p. 64)

Denis Smith, a Canadian liberal who has closely examined Ignatieff's justifications for the Kosovo War, notes that

> The evidence of failure is powerful: over a million refugees displaced, many civilians killed, the social and economic infrastructure of both Kosovo and Serbia wrecked, Milošević still in command of Serbia (though politically weakened), and a barely controlled new wave of ethnic cleansing underway in Kosovo (this time directed against the minority Serb population of the province). These are hardly minor events to be ignored when looking for useful lessons in the war or balancing the moral accounts.[3]

As we shall see, looking back and making empirical assessments of past interventions was not a specialty of the "cruise missile humanitarians." It turns out that there is always a next violent intervention to be advocated for using the emotive language of moral responsibility.

# 4 EMPIRE'S HANDMAIDEN IN IRAQ

*Human rights never justify permanent military occupation.*
—Michael Ignatieff, *Rights Revolution*

*Like some creep who thinks his honesty about being a creep is disarming, Ignatieff cooks up a testosterone-laced stew in which morsels of freedom and human rights are seasoned with crushing violence, enlightened greed, and calculated hypocrisy.*—Michael Neumann, "Apostle of He-manitarianism"

*Sometimes, hard as it is, the best thing to do is to do nothing: to let a victor emerge and then to assist him to establish and sustain the monopoly on violence upon which order depends. In the other case, where the adversaries are too evenly balanced to allow a decisive outcome, we may have to intervene on the side that appears to be most in the right and assist it to consolidate power. This means, of course, accepting that war may be an unavoidable solution to ethnic conflict. It means accepting a moral pact with the devil of war, seeking to use its flames to burn a path to peace.*—Michael Ignatieff, *The Warrior's Honour*

Ignatieff's third novel tells the story of an intrepid war reporter driven to vengeance after witnessing a horrific massacre. The world-weary protagonist Charlie Johnson, an aging correspondent covering the Balkan wars of the 1990s, is on assignment in a Kosovo village. Hiding in the woods, he observes Serb forces systematically rounding up and marching off all the men. Charlie watches as one brave, indignant young woman protests as her father is dragged away, and he stares impotently as a sadistic commander douses the woman in gasoline and sets her alight. Unable to do anything about the initial attack, after the Serbs depart Charlie desperately attempts to save the badly burned woman's life. He manages to keep her alive long enough for the medical cavalry to arrive, in the form of a US helicopter which airlifts her to a state-of-the-art trauma facility.

As two strapping US Navy medics expertly transfer the woman into the chopper, Charlie is filled with both gratitude and nostalgia for his own youth: "It was ridiculous, Charlie knew, but there he was, tears in his eyes, at the thought that they were safe in the arms of the empire" (CJF, p. 1). An hour later, Charlie waits in the field hospital for news of the patient; when the doctor finally arrives, it is to announce that the woman, whose name Charlie hadn't even learned, was dead. "For the rest of his life he was to wonder why he had ever allowed himself to believe it would end in any other way" (CJF, p. 12).

The war commentator had turned war novelist, and he was in no mood to say a farewell to arms. It could be argued that *Charlie Johnson in the Flames*, published in 2003, reflects a number of the conclusions Michael Ignatieff had reached from the Balkan wars of the 1990s. It also betrays his faith in western supremacy vis-à-vis "second-rate" peoples:

> [This] is not a novel about the Balkans. Ignatieff uses the region as a backdrop for reflections upon the nature of modern TV journalism, individual responsibility and the significance of what the British diplomat Robert Cooper has identified as liberal imperialism: to wit, military intervention in the name of humanitarian causes and democratic values. Ignatieff treats his Balkan characters sympathetically; however, their fundamental function is to fill

out the canvas, ensuring that the Anglo-Americans shine more brightly.[1]

In the novel, as in his non-fiction, Ignatieff gives us villains and victims, and the west and its armies have arrived too late to save the latter. But was the novel also a way of working through nagging doubts? After all, the Great Equivocator was in fine form in the closing paragraphs of *Virtual War*:

we need to reflect on the potential for self-righteous irrationality which lies hidden in abstractions like human rights. Those who supported the Kosovo war must face up to the unintended effects of moralizing the use of violence. For high-flown abstractions carry an inherent justification of everything done in their name. What is to prevent moral abstractions like human rights from inducing an absolutist frame of mind which, in defining all human rights violators as barbarians, legitimizes barbarism? (VW, p. 205)

Ignatieff never seriously re-examined the balance sheet in Kosovo. One way to immunize against the risks inherent in moralizing the application of state violence is to undertake detailed, empirical reporting and analysis of the impact of war and its aftermath. But Ignatieff never did this, although he did re-visit Kosovo a year after the NATO bombing, a trip he describes in his book *Empire Lite*, which was published in early 2003 "with an invasion of Iraq in prospect." In this slender volume, in which Ignatieff recounts visits to Bosnia, Kosovo, and Afghanistan, we find the explanation for his remarkably bellicose and unquestioning support for the upcoming invasion. Far from questioning his own moralizing in favor of war, with *Empire Lite* he was moving onward and upward to moralizing for imperialism writ large—elevating a subtext that had gained steam throughout his writings on the Balkans.

Ten years on, Kosovo remains a western protectorate, although formal independence was declared in 2009. In January 2010, NATO forces were cut by several thousand, down to approximately 10,000.

But Kosovo has a population of only slightly over two million, making it, relatively, much more intensively occupied by NATO than Afghanistan, even after Obama's significant escalations of that war. (The 2010 reductions, in fact, were justified in part to free up troops "for possible use in hotspots like Afghanistan or Iraq."[2]) The massive troop presence has nevertheless proven inadequate to protect Kosovo's minorities, and the threat of further ethnic cleansing still looms large. And, most inconveniently of all for the humanitarian warriors of the 1990s, there were the credible reports of links between the KLA and Islamist radical groups, perhaps even Al-Qaeda. After the mass murder of 9/11, this connection rendered any possible second thoughts on Kosovo downright embarrassing. So, not for the last time, the advocates of empire preferred to "look forward, not backward."[3]

## FIGHTING WORDS

It would be wrong to treat Ignatieff's judgment on Iraq merely as "a mistake"; in fact, it flowed inexorably from his near-total identification with US military power. In *Empire Lite*, Ignatieff takes up an old family business—propagandizing for imperialism. Lamentably, the good old days of his great grandfathers Nicholas Ignatieff and George Monro Grant were long gone, but the great-grandson still came out swinging: "Imperialism used to be the white man's burden. This gave it a bad reputation. But imperialism doesn't stop being necessary just because it becomes politically incorrect" (EL, p. 90).

*Empire Lite* is heavy on these sort of pithy, in-your-face, politically incorrect phrases. No effete, overly intellectual constructions from this teller of hard truths. Ignatieff sought to rouse the complacent American liberal conscience to its historical duty.

> America's entire war on terror is an exercise in imperialism. This may come as a shock to Americans, who don't like to think of their country as an empire. But what else can you call America's legions of soldiers, spooks and Special Forces straddling the globe? These

garrisons are by no means temporary. Terror can't be controlled unless order is built in the anarchic zones where terrorists find shelter.

There were plenty of new battles to be fought—weak-kneed fools be damned. And the new rationales for military intervention that Ignatieff and others had been road-testing in the 1990s were more sought-after commodities than ever before. Some of his more specific "rules" of intervention, designed to fit the Balkan context, would just have to be ignored. Newly ensconced at Harvard, Ignatieff was well positioned to be in the frontline of the battle of ideas over the war on terror.

In the early days after 9/11, Ignatieff was quick to stake out a hawkish position, writing in the *Guardian* that the terror attacks on the United States were an act of "apocalyptic nihilism," outside the realm of politics.[4] Those who believed that "the terrorists' hatreds must be understood, and that what they hate must be changed so that they will hate no more" were dismissed as naïve and foolhardy. "Since the politics of reason cannot defeat apocalyptic nihilism, we must fight," he thundered.

He sketched an impressionistic political history of this non-political taxonomic invention ("apocalyptic nihilism"), beginning with a "purely secular variant" in the form of the nineteenth century Russian anarchists, the Narodniks: "The liberator tsar was struck down in St. Petersburg in 1881, and apocalyptic nihilism celebrated its first triumph, but not its last." Ignatieff credits "the same" nihilism—and yet somehow different, "this time in the form of an all-consuming hatred of bourgeois society"—with drawing recruits to fascism and communism in the 1930s. From the anarchists to the communists and Nazis to Al-Qaeda—an unbroken continuity of apocalyptic nihilism? The audacity is in the sheer incoherence. But all these muddled and conflated historical references are nevertheless marshaled with a purpose: to remind the reader that nihilism cannot be talked to or negotiated with—only killed. To harbor doubts about bombing Serbia was to risk appeasing the new Hitler, but to question invasions and new wars intended to root out Al-Qaeda was to appease Hitler, Stalin, and Charlie Manson all at once.

Ignatieff is not the only writer to have drawn analogies between Al-Qaeda and nineteenth-century anarchism, but in his case there is an ironic personal connection that in fact undermines his own platitudinous history of nihilism. After Czar Alexander II was assassinated, it was Ignatieff's own great-grandfather, the vicious anti-Semite Nicholas, who as Minister of the Interior imposed a sweeping series of repressive "Extraordinary and Temporary Measures." In *The Russian Album*, the great-grandson explains that these laws

> gave provincial governors the power to suspend normal legal procedure and individual civil rights wherever a strike, an attack or a riot required it. The decree also empowered the government to hand suspects over to summary court martial, to order house arrests and domestic searches, and to outlaw any meetings, close any institution, or suspend any newspaper as it saw fit. Until 1917, these measures were to remain the key statutes of the autocracy, its chief legal weapon in its losing struggle for survival. It was from their heavy hand that the young Lenin and Stalin were to acquire their contempt for legality and due process. (RA, p. 56)

In other words, Ignatieff himself asserts that communism—in its Russian variant, at least—can be understood with reference to the actual history which conditioned its development. His explanation posits an incipient authoritarianism in Russian socialism born not of the Bolsheviks' amorality but rather of the immorality of the retrograde measures imposed by his own ancestor. Setting aside Ignatieff's speculative personal psychological explanations, there's a lesson here that militates against the dichotomy at the dark heart of his "lesser evil" framework. The evils of two contending systems exist in a complex relationship, sometimes causal, sometimes symbiotic—but rarely if ever in easily qualitatively differentiated "greater" and "lesser."

The fact that Ignatieff's sketch of the "continuity" of apocalyptic nihilism begins with the regicidal Russian bomb-throwers betrays his solipsistic tendencies. It's worth noting that Nicholas Ignatieff's "extraordinary measures" were justified by Jew-hatred and exacerbated its prevalence in the Russian Empire. Though certainly not on the same scale as the mass emigrations, ethnic cleansings, and pogroms of nineteenth-century Russia, the "extraordinary" measures that Michael Ignatieff would endorse post-9/11 were as intrinsically linked to Islamophobia as his great-grandfather's were to anti-Semitism.

In the same article, while sketching a highly dubious history of terrorism to bolster his arguments for war, Ignatieff warns against historical analysis by those more critical of a violent response. He makes a preemptive strike on any who would seek to locate the causes of anti-US terrorism in the actual history and foreign policy of the United States:

> It is an adolescent fantasy to assign the injustice of the world to a single address. It is also an indulgence to enjoy the freedoms of western societies while blaming these societies for the world's evils. A guilty conscience can make idiots of us all. The idiocy is to assume that the terrorists represent anybody other than their own criminal designs.

There can be no appeasement of these criminals, he maintains. In fact, Ignatieff repeats, "there is no possible political response to apocalyptic nihilism." That leaves only a long, violent conflagration, one that is bound to be a "dirty war." For the sake of the consciences of those who fight in our name, and for the sake of the "moral identity that gives justice to the cause," we should avoid excessive brutality in this effort. After a bellicose call to arms, bracing his high-minded readers for the vicissitudes of protracted struggle, Ignatieff closes the article with a call for a "discriminate, proportional and restrained" war against terror.

The jab about the "adolescent fantasy" of blaming the US for "the injustices of the world" was an infantile red herring. The reality was that those sounding doubtful, cautious or outright oppositional notes in the weeks between 9/11 and the bombing of Afghanistan repeatedly cited historical precedent from other countries, and noted that the logic of the "war on terror" would be invoked by other states seeking to justify repressive and expansionist policies.

Christopher Hitchens wrote of 9/11 as the day that US society woke up from its complacency in the face of enemies, "the day when that realm of illusion was dispelled."[5] Ignatieff too had high hopes that the false consciousness of liberals who refused to comprehend their imperial duties would fall along with the twin towers:

"There might be reason, even though the awakening has been brutal, to be thankful to the barbarians. After all, they are, as the poet Celan said, a kind of solution. They have offered the empire a new raison d'être and a long-term strategic objective: the global eradication of terror" (EL, p. 5).

Little seemed to restrain the now US-based warrior-scholar. He was becoming more aggressive in his assertions, less reflective, less nuanced. This made him a great tool for an administration thinking well ahead and beyond the coming strike against Afghanistan. Although the bombs started falling on Afghanistan on October 7, 2001, the primary target of the war machine was already Saddam Hussein's Iraqi regime. Former US anti-terror czar Richard Clarke famously told of President Bush pulling him aside on September 12, 2001 and "testily" instructing him to find links between Al-Qaeda and Iraq.[6] There were no such links, no Iraqi passports among the 19 hijackers, no smoking gun pointing to Baghdad whatsoever. In the absence of any such evidence, the warmonger intellectuals had an important role to play, especially in rallying liberal opinion.

## ON THE ROAD TO WAR IN IRAQ

"Timidity is not prudence; it is a confession of weakness." Thus wrote Michael Ignatieff in a *New York Times Magazine* cover story of January 5, 2003, declaring his support for George W. Bush's pending invasion of Iraq.[7] The bulky 7,000-plus-word cover story projected both strength and audacity: "The American Empire (Get Used To It)." Ignatieff's text was unwieldy and self-contradictory in parts, but his argument was less qualified and caveat-littered than usual. A talented mimic, just over two years after moving to the US the understated essayist of the *London Review of Books* had morphed into a telling-it-like-it-is Yank. "Get used to it" was a liberal's belligerent echo of George W. Bush's "Bring it on." As with Blair in the previous decade, Ignatieff was reflecting the president's catchphrases and talking points. If his declaration of war shocked some colleagues and liberal opinion generally, so be it. This was his story, after all, and he would make it up as he went along.

There was plenty in the article to shock and awe. Gone were the ironic, philosophical musings about our "post-imperial" age:

> what word but "empire" describes the awesome thing that America is becoming? It is the only nation that police[s] the world through five global military commands; maintains more than a million men and women at arms on four continents; deploys carrier battle groups on watch in every ocean; guarantees the survival of countries from Israel to South Korea; drives the wheels of global trade and commerce; and fills the hearts and minds of an entire planet with its dreams and desires.

*Awesome.* So awesome, so exceptional, in fact, that the empire could openly flaunt its self-interest in the face of the international community, "laying down the rules America wants (on everything from markets to weapons of mass destruction) while exempting itself from other rules (the Kyoto Protocol on climate change and the International Criminal Court) that go against its interest."

Casting international law, cooperation, and negotiation to the wind, Ignatieff then throws the United Nations under the bus, with a downright rabid metaphor worthy of Fox News:

The United Nations lay dozing like a dog before the fire, happy to ignore Saddam, until an American president seized it by the scruff of the neck and made it bark. Multilateral solutions to the world's problems are all very well, but they have no teeth unless America bares its fangs.

One doesn't know where to start with this distastefully aggressive metaphor. It's true that the Kyoto Accord had no teeth and no impact, mostly because America lay dozing before the fire of climate change. Invoking a befanged America in a pro-imperialist rant? Somebody take a stake to the heart of this essay! But Ignatieff's ode to empire was far from over. It was approaching a crescendo:

> America's empire is not like empires of times past, built on colonies, conquest and the white man's burden ... The 21st century imperium is a new invention in the annals of political science, an empire lite, a global hegemony whose grace notes are free markets, human rights and democracy, enforced by the most awesome military power the world has ever known.

Chomsky, as it happens, was asked about this particular passage in an interview with David Barsamian, and responded:

> Of course, the apologists for every other imperial power have said the same thing. So you can go back to John Stuart Mill ... He defended the British Empire in very much those words. John Stuart Mill wrote the classic essay on humanitarian intervention. Everyone studies it in law schools. What he says is, Britain is unique in the world. It's unlike any country before it. Other countries have crass motives and seek gain and so on, but the British act only for the benefit of others ... But everything we do is for the benefit of the natives, the barbarians. We want to bring them free markets and honest rule and freedom and all kinds of wonderful things. Today's version is just illustrating Marx's comment about tragedy being repeated as farce ... I'm surprised that Ignatieff is not aware that he's just repeating a very familiar rhetoric.[8]

Barsamian then brought up the *New York Times*'s Thomas Friedman, who was at least more honest than Ignatieff about the relationship between the grace notes of a "free market" and the "awesome" military might of the United States: "The hidden hand of the market will never work without a hidden fist. McDonald's cannot flourish without McDonnell Douglas, the designer of the F-15. And the hidden fist that keeps the world safe for Silicon Valley's technologies to flourish is called the US Army, Air Force, Navy and Marine Corps."[9]

Having reached the heights of imperial ecstasy, Ignatieff comes down a bit, surveying part of the United States' history of messianic imperialism going back to Woodrow Wilson after Versailles. He could have gone back further. Many have convincingly argued that the American empire was present from the earliest days of the Republic, long before the Spanish-American War at the end of the nineteenth-century that saw Cuba and the Philippines fall "like ripe fruit" into US control. Chomsky, for one, has argued that the Seminole War—the brutal conquest of Florida—was justified on grounds comparable to the Bush Doctrine of preemptive war.[10]

Too much history, however, would take away from the gravitas of the "moment of truth," as Ignatieff understood the Iraq invasion. And don't think for a second that he had not considered the risks of an imperial war: "What empires lavish abroad," he wrote,

thcy cannot spend on good republican government at home: on hospitals or roads or schools ... A republic that has paid a tiny burden to maintain its empire—no more than about 4 percent of its gross domestic product—now contemplates a bill that is altogether steeper. Even if victory is rapid, a war in Iraq and a postwar occupation may cost anywhere from $120 billion to $200 billion ... To call America the new Rome is at once to recall Rome's glory and its eventual fate at the hands of the barbarians. A confident and carefree republic ... now has to confront not just an unending imperial destiny but also a remote possibility that seems to haunt the history of empire: hubris followed by defeat.

Having parsed the dangers and stared the ghosts of empire in the face, Ignatieff then urges his readers to join the war party, adopting whole hog the fear-mongering of the Bush administration. Invoking the threat of rogue states like Iraq relaying WMDs to "a terrorist internationale"—is this a nod to the anarcho-communist faction in his idiosyncratic theory of apocalyptic nihilism?—he states that this war will be "the first in a series of struggles" to prevent the proliferation of WMDs falling into the hands of a "global terrorist network" (just in case we didn't understand the French word for international). In giving up on containment, the Bush administration was "not unreasonable," Ignatieff asserted, because containment was "not designed to stop production of sarin, VX nerve gas, anthrax and nuclear weapons." With visions of mushroom clouds dancing in his readers' heads, Ignatieff tells them that "regime change" is necessary, although only as "reluctant last resort."

It is worth noting here that not only does Ignatieff unquestioningly repeat and even embellish the administration's WMD claims—lies that were being loudly refuted at the time by the likes of former head UN weapons inspector, Scott Ritter, among others—but he also plays up the canard of Saddam Hussein smuggling a nuke to his, Hussein's, hated enemy, Osama Bin Laden. This is pure horror-fantasy, and it is impossible to imagine that Ignatieff was ignorant enough to have been unaware of the bitter animosity between the leadership of Al-Qaeda and the secular authoritarians of Baghdad.

Having clearly sided with the war-makers, Ignatieff focuses on a key theme of *Empire Lite*: imperialists have to be in it for the long haul. This is particularly the case in Iraq because the invasion was merely an opening salvo in the "reordering of the entire region." For starters, and converging perfectly with the delusions of the neo-conservatives, Ignatieff projects a future Middle East where Syria "will be coaxed" into giving up their claim to the Israeli occupied Golan Heights; where the Kurds will accept a Kurdistan that doesn't infringe of the borders of their primary oppressors, the Turks; and where, by some strange alchemy, the illegal invasion of Iraq will lead to democratization in Saudi Arabia. He does, however, take off his rose-colored glasses when it comes to Israel, observing correctly that "[u]nseating an Arab government in Iraq while leaving the Palestinians to face Israeli tanks and helicopter gunships is a virtual guarantee of unending Islamic wrath against the United States." This sort of realism on the Middle East would only finally be beaten out of Ignatieff in later years, through the discipline of the Israel lobby in Canada.

Having made the case for war and predicted a virtuous domino effect, Ignatieff next turns to the challenges facing the US imperial project. The Europeans are not pleased with their secondary role, and many of them share the outrage of human rights advocates who see US actions as blatantly self-serving. He points out that successive US governments have signed up to international treaties and organizations only when it suits them, while seeking to undermine others, such as the Kyoto Protocol and the International Criminal Court, which go against their imperial interests. Like it or not, "the empire will not be tied down like Gulliver with a thousand legal strings." The United States, Ignatieff argues, "enforces a new division of labor in which America does the fighting, the French, British and Germans do the police patrols in the border zones and the Dutch, Swiss and Scandinavians provide the humanitarian aid." (The Canadians here don't warrant a mention, despite Ignatieff's true, patriot love.)

Ignatieff even raises the specter of Vietnam, admitting that the invasion of Iraq "will rouse the nationalist passions of people [across the Islamic world] who want to rule themselves and worship as they please." He even concedes that, "[a]s Vietnam shows, empire is no match, long-term, for nationalism." Was this a betrayal of the essay's thesis, or did this sentence merely throw into relief the author's own confusion?

In a response to one of his sharpest critics, just as his book *Empire Lite* was being published a few months later, Ignatieff claimed that his *Times Magazine* essay did not in fact endorse the US empire.

In the March 2003 issue of *Harper's*, then-editor Lewis Lapham had assailed Ignatieff for his "sententious and vacant prose, most of it indistinguishable from the ad copy for an Armani scarf or a Ferragamo shoe," in a furious piece decrying the war in Iraq and the intellectual culture that had allowed it to take place. Lapham lumps Ignatieff in with the rest of the Beltway bombers:

> [neither] does he say anything that hasn't been said repeatedly over the last nine months, by the cadre of Washington propagandists ... Be not timid, do not flinch. Shoulder the burden of civilization and its discontents. Lift from the continents of Africa and Asia the weight of despotic evildoers. Know that if America does the fighting other people will do the dying. Learn to appreciate the refined elegance (conceptually minimalist, gracefully postmodern) of high-altitude precision bombing ..."[11]

In a published letter to the editor, Ignatieff responded by claiming that Lapham had "[mistaken] description for endorsement," adding that "no imperial power can withstand the power of modern nationalism, the desire of people to free themselves from foreign interference."[12] However, even the most cursory of inspections of *Empire Lite* and Ignatieff's other subsequent writing on Iraq and empire makes a mockery of the assertion that he was misunderstood.

His high-profile support for the war certainly angered many colleagues, and his support for encroachments on civil liberties in the name of the war on terror only made things worse. His book *The Lesser Evil* came out in 2004, the same year that the horrific images from Abu Ghraib prison were circulated all over the world. In a speech in late 2004, Ignatieff made an astounding assertion about the torture scandal in Iraq, effectively blaming the victims: "the terrorists are controlling the escalation gradient: provoking US interrogators into the abuses at Abu Ghraib, drawing them into cities like Najaf and Falluja."[13] Ignatieff offered no evidence that suggested the victims of US torture and abuse in

Iraq had "provoked" the occupiers, and this particular claim was not repeated.

In *The Lesser Evil*, Ignatieff considers how the liberal democracies should respond to terrorism. He provides some substantial, and useful, sketches of how societies from Britain to Sri Lanka have responded to political terrorism. Superficially, his argument is for prudent, minimalist state responses to terror. What might otherwise have been a nuanced and usefully cautionary study, however, is distorted by Ignatieff's identification with imperialism. This leads him to blur his categories of lesser (liberal democracy) and greater evils ("nihilistic" terrorism) into the usual tropes justifying western domination and neo-colonialism, eliding altogether the key point that empire and terrorism are often symbiotic processes. The failure of lesser nations and peoples, Ignatieff asserts, is nothing whatsoever to do with the greatness of the most powerful liberal democracies: "our success is not a fact to feel guilty about, and the failure of other societies is not our fault" (LE, p. 168).

So it is that what seems to be a prescription for reason and restraint blurs into a defense of the most irrational and unrestrained foreign policy. Ignatieff, at points, writes about "Evil" the way George W. Bush speaks about it: "free peoples used to living at peace have difficulty admitting that they are actually faced with evil" (LE, p. 167). Once again, Ignatieff seems to be trying to rouse his complacent fellow liberals to arms.

*The Lesser Evil* disavows torture, but with a caveat allowing for all kinds of abusive actions that could well be called torture. After advocating "an outright ban on torture," Ignatieff asserts that legislation is needed to "define acceptable degrees of coercive interrogation." "Permissible duress might include forms of sleep deprivation that do not result in lasting harm to mental or physical health, together with disinformation and disorientation (like keeping prisoners in hoods) that would produce stress."[14] This line of argument led to sharp denunciations. Laurie Taylor, writing in *New Humanist*, summarized Ignatieff's feud with Conor Gearty, who included Ignatieff among "torture's new best friends." He recaps the case made by Gearty and others against Ignatieff's line of reasoning:

> Ignatieff is the best exemplar of this type of intellectual because of his apparently total commitment to the idea that we are now faced with "evil" people and that unless we fight evil with evil we will succumb. It is precisely because we are democratic and special that, in Ignatieff's words "necessity may require us to take actions in defence of democracy which will stray from democracy's own foundational commitments to dignity." So occasional lapses in human rights can be excused as lesser evils.[15]

## MEANWHILE BACK IN CANADA

While Ignatieff was busy urging on the Iraq War, back in Canada a very different scene was playing out. The ranks of the anti-war movement were swelling, the numbers mushrooming with each demonstration. On February 15, 2003, the largest globally coordinated day of protest took place, with more than 10 million participating worldwide. Tens of thousands rallied in many Canadian cities. More than 100,000 marched in Montreal, Quebec, where anti-war sentiment was traditionally highest. Briefly, both globally and in Canada, anti-war sentiment was manifest in the streets in what looked like the beginnings of a powerful social movement. The new NDP leader Jack Layton effectively linked his party with the movement, using media appearances to urge Canadians to join in the peace rallies.

Then Liberal Prime Minister Jean Chrétien surveyed this landscape and made a shrewd decision, one he would later trumpet as a key part of his legacy. Chrétien had the kind of populist touch that Ignatieff can only dream of, and he also had impeccable instincts for political survival. He knew, in particular, that openly supporting the US would spark outrage, especially in Quebec. As he tells it, one last request was made for Canada to join the "coalition of the willing" in invading Iraq, delivered on March 17, 2003, the morning before the war began. The request did not come from Washington, but rather from the British government led by Tony Blair. Instead of phoning in his regrets to the White House, Chrétien rose in the House of Commons to make his announcement: Canada would not join the list of invaders. The Liberal government would, shortly thereafter, "mend fences" with the US administration by bolstering Canadian troop levels in Afghanistan, and by cooperating in backing the 2004 coup d'état in Haiti. Canada would also magnanimously provide funds to train the new Iraqi police forces, a ship to escort war-bound traffic in the Persian Gulf, and some of its top officers to serve on exchange in command of US forces. Canadian Lt.-Gen. Walt Natynczyk, for instance, was in charge of 30,000 troops in Iraq. In 2008, Natynczyk was named head of the Canadian Forces (CF)—a promotion hailed by top US military officials.[16] Both Natynczyk and his predecessor Rick Hillier had attended officer training in Fort Hood, Texas—a sort of School of the Americas for Canada, apparently.

Stephen Harper was leader of the opposition at the time of the Iraq invasion. He and colleague Stockwell Day co-signed a letter in the *Wall Street Journal*. They bemoaned Chrétien's decision and pledged their allegiance to the US war: "[we support] the American and British position because we share their concerns, their worries about the future if Iraq is left unattended to, and their fundamental vision of civilization and human values ... In our hearts and minds, we will be with our allies and friends. And Canadians will be overwhelmingly with us."[17] Harper took his pro-war message to Fox News, where he claimed that, contrary to the evidence of the peace-mongering mobs in the streets, "Outside of Quebec, I believe very strongly the silent majority of Canadians is strongly supportive."[18]

Not content with disparaging Canada's decision on Iraq in the US right-wing's favored media outlets, Harper also rose in the Canadian Parliament to speak out against the weak-kneed pacifism of his compatriots. Many of the Bush administration's fellow travelers were rising in their respective halls of government to tout the American war. One of them was Australia's John Howard.

A March 13, 2003 speech by Howard justifying Australia's joining the "coalition of the willing" warned that:

> As the possession of weapons of mass destruction spreads, so the danger of such weapons coming into the hands of terrorist groups will multiply. That is the ultimate nightmare which the world must take decisive and effective steps to prevent. Possession of chemical, biological or nuclear weapons by terrorists would constitute a direct, undeniable and lethal threat to Australia and its people.[19]

Two days later, on March 20, 2003, Harper spoke in the House of Commons decrying Canada's snubbing of the coalition of the killing. More than an echo of Howard, Harper's speech sounded close to being a tape recording:

> As the possession of weapons of mass destruction spreads, the danger of such weapons coming into the hands of terrorist groups will multiply, particularly given in this case the shameless association of Iraq with rogue non-state organizations. That is the ultimate nightmare which the world must take decisive and effective steps to prevent. Possession of chemical, biological or nuclear weapons by terrorists would constitute a direct, undeniable and lethal threat to the world, including to Canada and its people.[20]

Within a year, Harper's support for the Iraq War would fade and then retroactively disappear, faced with the overwhelming opposition of the public—some polls showing as many as 80 percent of Canadians against the war—and the discipline imposed by a forthcoming election. By April 2004, although still wanting the US to "succeed" in Iraq, Harper was saying that it wouldn't be "feasible" to send Canadian troops to aid the war effort. By June of that year, in the midst of a close election race, Harper twisted logic and defied credulity by asserting that he had really just wanted a "predeployment" of Canadian troops to Iraq, which could have in fact helped achieve peace. "It was about putting pressure on Saddam to comply with UN resolutions and I continue to believe if allies had acted in a concerted measure to put that pressure, we could have avoided a war."[21]

The other tack Harper took was that Canada's military was/is so ill-equipped and undermanned that there would not have been any question of Canadian troops being deployed to Iraq anyway. For all his eerie calm and Ken-doll hair, even Harper couldn't sell this spin, and he went on to lose in his first national election campaign as party leader. Two election campaigns later, in 2008, the Liberals exposed the Howard-Harper speech, forcing a Harper speechwriter to resign, and admit to the plagiarism.[22] The Liberals made good use of the scandal to dredge up Harper's support for Bush's war, forcing Harper to admit during a televised leaders' debate that the Iraq War was "absolutely an error."[23]

## EMPIRE'S HANDMAIDEN

In contrast to Harper's early step back from his vociferous support for the Iraq invasion, Ignatieff waded in further before—finally— admitting his error in 2007. To understand his stubbornness on the matter, it's worth sampling several of his post-invasion writings and looking more closely at his arguments in *Empire Lite*. A glance at the quotation on the book's front cover suggests that Lapham had not failed to appreciate the nuance of Ignatieff's prose: "Nobody likes empires, but there are some problems for which there are only imperial solutions." The real thesis of the book is the opposite of what is suggested by its title. Ignatieff seeks not only to describe the empire to a US elite reluctant to openly admit its existence; he also seeks to rouse them from their dozing complacence to the reality that imperialism involves a serious and sustained investment of blood, treasure, and time. He has no patience with half measures against the "barbarians"; today's Rome must be willing to garrison the "frontier zones" for as long as it takes. "Empires that do not demonstrate inflexible determination do not survive" (EL, p.1).

Ignatieff hammered this theme home in a 2003 piece in the *New York Times Magazine*, "Why Are We In Iraq? (And Liberia?

And Afghanistan?)."[24] Already, the putative liberators of Iraq were facing armed resistance, while at home the fairy tale of WMDs was unraveling. Paul Wolfowitz, one of the most crazed and ideological of the neo-conservatives in the US administration, had been forced to admit that the intelligence on WMDs had been "murky." Ignatieff, in turn, admonished him—"If so, the American people should have been told just that"—without taking responsibility for the absolute credulity with which he had participated in the murky fear-mongering which had led to war. Ignatieff goes further, openly stating that the war was sold to the public on false pretenses:

> much mention was made of human rights and democracy and much less about the obvious fact the operation was about oil, not in the callow sense of going to war for the sake of Halliburton but in the wider sense of America's consolidating its hegemonic role as the guarantor of stable oil supplies for the Western economy.

Putting it another way, he admits that the WMDs were only the "bureaucratic" reason for the war, not the real reason. Despite this, Ignatieff still finds himself supporting the war, appearing to argue that the false justifications were permissible since the invasion resulted in the removal of an odious regime: "If the consequence of intervention is a rights-respecting Iraq in a decade or so, who cares whether the intentions that led to it were mixed at best?"

Returning to the venture which inspired Kipling's "White Man's Burden," Ignatieff even draws an analogy between Iraq and the US conquest of the Philippines, another intervention which was "unilateral, opposed by most of the world [and] an act of territorial conquest." Although the US occupation "may not have done much for the Philippines … it did a lot to make America a leading power in the Pacific." Ignatieff thinks Iraq offers a "geostrategic benefit on the same scale." The blood price of these two US wars is comparable: in the Philippines over 4,000 US dead and hundreds of thousands of Filipinos; in Iraq, to date, over 5,000 US dead and over a million Iraqis. At the time, however, things were looking so rosy that Ignatieff asserted that "intervention is getting cheaper." Overstretch was not "a very real constraint on America's propensity to intervene."

From this optimistic perspective, only two potential nuisances remained to restrain the "American Goliath": the peace movement in the Belly of the Beast, and a meddlesome and resentful international community. Ignatieff presents a counter-factual history to dismiss the former, and offers a proposal for UN reform in order to co-opt the latter.

The "anti-intervention party in US politics," Ignatieff claims, "often captures the high moral ground but usually loses the war for public opinion." He asserts that Vietnam was the "single exception" where the majority became convinced that the country could "lose its soul" overseas. He goes further, claiming, as noted above, that not only are interventions "getting cheaper," but that they "are popular, and they remain popular even if American soldiers die."

On this point, it would take a couple years and the deaths of several thousand US soldiers to prove Ignatieff wrong. The ultimate unpopularity and abject failure of the Iraq War would contribute to damaging his academic reputation and stalling his leadership aspirations once he had fled Harvard for Canadian politics. Even after an admission of his great mistake, the stain of the Iraq War has proved difficult for Ignatieff to wash away.

Michael Ignatieff might now wonder how he could have convinced himself it would end any other way.

# 5 DON'T TALK ABOUT PALESTINE

I was once out for drinks with a friend of a friend, when my new acquaintance turned the conversation to politics. He was a Liberal, who had apparently worked on some big-time campaigns in the recent past. I think he was bemused by my earnest leftism, because he soon launched into an ostensibly humorous monologue about the "top five ways the Left could actually win elections." The list was mostly forgettable stuff (not so much how to win an election as how to become a Liberal), but there was one point on which I remember his adamant insistence. *Don't talk about Palestine!* The corollary to this, of course, was *don't criticize Israel!* As he elaborated on it, the point was not that there was anything unworthy about the struggle against occupation in Palestine. Rather, that it was politically risky to let on that you knew this, and political suicide to reveal that you cared.

As we will see a little later, Michael Ignatieff learned this lesson the hard way in his rookie year in Canadian politics. But he was a quick student, and within a few years his response had matured on questions related to the Middle East, moving from simple self-censorship to outright attack against those who dared to talk about Palestine.

In March 2009 Ignatieff published an op-ed in the *National Post*[1] in which he traduced the organizers of "Israeli Apartheid Week," an annual event in support of Palestinian human rights and critical of Israeli policies that had been growing in size and scope on Canadian campuses. The *Post* is normally hostile territory for a Liberal leader, but in this case they were happy to provide the column space.

Ignatieff started off with some good old bipartisan Canadian bromides, the better to level his accusation:

> We respect differences—of opinion, nationality, race and creed. We abandon that respect at our peril. "Israel Apartheid Week" (IAW), now underway on university campuses across Canada, betrays the values of mutual respect that Canada has always promoted.

He then unleashed a flurry of non-sequiturs:

> International law defines "apartheid" as a crime against human-ity. Labeling Israel as an "apartheid" state is a deliberate attempt to undermine the legitimacy of the Jewish state itself. Criticism of Israel is legitimate. Attempting to describe its very existence as a crime against humanity is not.

He adds to this the extremely serious charge that IAW represents a "demonization" which "targets institutions and individuals because of what and who they are—Israeli and Jewish." He further goes on to assert, without providing any specific examples or testi-mony, that IAW has left Jewish students intimidated to the point of being "afraid to express their opinions." The last half of the op-ed is devoted to attacking the Ontario branch of the Canadian Union of Public Employees for passing a resolution in favor of the inter-national campaign for Boycott, Divestment and Sanctions against Israel, part of what Ignatieff calls a "chorus of denunciation of Israel" which "threatens academic freedom" and "free exchange."

In March 2010, Ignatieff again issued a similar denunciation of Apartheid Week. He claimed that Jewish students on campus were "physically threatened," charging the organizers with "an attempt to heighten the tensions in our communities around the tragic conflict in the Middle East."[2]

This charge of racism, especially of such a pernicious and historically deadly variety, is most serious indeed. And it is entirely baseless, flowing only from Ignatieff's own logical fallacy about describing Israel with the word apartheid. Given Ignatieff's own record, the denunciation also amounted to a display of almost superhuman chutzpah. For someone whose published work had soft-pedaled on his own great-grandfather's anti-Semitism and contributions to the worst anti-Jewish violence prior to the Nazi Holocaust, one would think Ignatieff might have treaded this ground more carefully. But, as with the Ukrainians (or "little Russians," as Ignatieff's family always called them), Ignatieff is quick to smear others with allegations of hatred of the Jewish people.

The charge of racism rests first on the equation of the state of Israel with the Jewish people as a whole. This conflation is a common and transparent device used to stifle honest discussion of the Middle East. The second pillar upon which Ignatieff's allegation rests is the use of the term "apartheid" to describe the actions of the state of Israel. Although the analogy is certainly not perfect—it is after all an *analogy*—many respected human rights activists, scholars, and political leaders have used the term to describe Israel and its actions in the occupied territories. Some of those who have spoken of apartheid and Israel in the same breath have done so with unquestioned moral authority. These include Ronnie Kasrils, the Jewish South African anti-apartheid fighter and former minister in the post-apartheid government, as well as Nelson Mandela and Archbishop Desmond Tutu themselves. Here is Tutu,writing in 2002:

> The end of apartheid stands as one of the crowning accomplishments of the past century, but we would not have succeeded without the help of international pressure—in particular the divestment movement of the 1980s. Over the past six months a similar movement has taken shape, this time aiming at an end to the Israeli occupation ... Yesterday's South African township dwellers can tell

you about today's life in the occupied territories. To travel only blocks in his own homeland, a grandfather waits on the whim of a teenage soldier. More than an emergency is needed to get to a hospital; less than a crime earns a trip to jail. The lucky ones have a permit to leave their squalor to work in Israel's cities, but their luck runs out when security closes all checkpoints, paralyzing an entire people. The indignities, dependence and anger are all too familiar.[3]

Tutu and those who lived through the indignities in apartheid South Africa's townships, however, were not the only ones to see an analogy and to state it publicly. Here are the opening lines of a *Guardian* column by Michael Ignatieff, which appeared in 2002, a couple of months before Tutu's piece:

Two years ago, an American friend took me on a helicopter ride from Jerusalem to the Golan Heights over the Palestinian West Bank. He wanted to show me how vulnerable Israel was, how the Arabs only had to cross 11km of land to reach the sea and throw the Israelis into it. I got this message but I also came away with another one. When I looked down at the West Bank, at the settlements like Crusader forts occupying the high ground, at the Israeli security cordon along the Jordan river closing off the Palestinian lands from Jordan, I knew I was not looking down at a state or the beginnings of one, but at a Bantustan, one of those pseudo-states created in the dying years of apartheid to keep the African population under control.

This was not a one-time flourish, either. In *Empire Lite*, Ignatieff admits, "[America] is hated both because it is Israel's mainstay and because even when it supports Palestinian statehood, it gives them no more than a Bantustan." The "sham state" created by the Oslo process made Palestinian revolt "inevitable," since it "was divided by roads and settlements, split into the West Bank and Gaza and incapable of effective self-rule and development" (EL, p. 9).

Speaking to a Toronto audience in 2004, Ignatieff reminded his audience, "Israel must bear some portion of the responsibility for destroying its partner for peace."[4]

He stated that the continuing negation of Palestinian rights by Israel would be "a powerful recruiting sergeant for jihadis" in the Holy Land and beyond. Criticizing the settlements and the annexation of territory that accompanied the construction of a massive, misnamed "security fence" through the West Bank, Ignatieff presciently saw the writing on the apartheid wall:

> the Sharon plan effectively bids farewell to the two-state solution as a political strategy for reducing terror attacks against Israel. It replaces the two-state solution with a new strategy—one aimed at unilateral withdrawal, territorial separation, and the cantonization of the Palestinian population in a territory so divided and so encircled that it is simply not viable as a state … Sealing the Palestinians in one Bantustan, called Gaza, and four other cantons on the West Bank will create a permanent terrorist haven on the borders of Israel.[5]

Although he condemned the violent resistance of Palestinians to their oppression, he concedes in his book *The Lesser Evil* that in the West Bank or Gaza his arguments for non-violence would be heard "as a strategy to keep the weak in submission and confirm the privileges of the strong." He writes that non-violence at this stage in the game might mean surrendering to Israeli imposed apartheid: "Calling on Palestinians to return to the path of deliberative nonviolence might be to condemn them to a Palestine reduced to the size of a Bantustan" (LE, p. 90). It should be noted that Ignatieff was well aware of the horrors of the original Bantustans in South Africa, and of the system of segregation and oppression of which they were a lynchpin. In 2001, he wrote the introduction to the book *Truth and Lies: Stories From the Truth and Reconciliation Commission in South Africa*, published by Granta Books.

By Ignatieff's criteria, as laid out in his indictment of Israeli Apartheid Week, he is guilty of anti-Semitism by comparing Israel with a regime that he defines as having been guilty of crimes against humanity. In fact, he made his apartheid analogy in the pages of one of the most influential publications in the world, before the designation "Israeli apartheid" had become commonplace even in the milieu of Palestine solidarity organizing. If activism around the slogan of Israeli apartheid is racist, then he is a trailblazing anti-Semite.

When assessing Ignatieff's written record on Palestine, I frankly wonder if he has any sort of moral center whatsoever. It's not that one can never genuinely change one's mind, it's just there is no trace at all of the humility or regret that would normally accompany such an about face. I think back to his Iraq mea culpa, which on closer reading was no such thing all. In it, in fact, he more or less openly admitted his own bad faith. Politics is theatre, he asserted, and so politicians are really actors who have to feign indignation and other emotions they do not feel. Academics, for their part, merely play with words and pursue digressions with ideas for their own sake because they are detached from the real world consequences that politicians must anticipate. With his own position on Israel-Palestine having bobbled all over the place, what did Ignatieff really believe? Had he changed his opinion close to 180 degrees, or was he just a self-incriminating hypocrite? Or, was it all an act? Did he believe *anything* he ever said or wrote?

One thing Ignatieff does believe in is power, and in that I think lies the best explanation for how, in less than a decade, he went from being someone willing to tell hard truths about Israel to someone willing to publicly slander the truth-tellers.

Back in 2002, Ignatieff linked his support for US invasion and occupation with strong recommendations for an end to Israel's occupation and colonization of the West Bank and Gaza: "It is time to say that all but those settlements right on the 1967 green line must go."[6] Although he argued that the Palestinian refugees' right of return should be "extinguished with a cash settlement," he also stated that a one-state solution "would be an excellent idea"— except for the fact, he says, that it wasn't what either side wanted.

Ignatieff's preferred two-state solution would not be brought about merely by political or economic pressure; in his view, the "US [must] commit its own troops, and those of willing allies, not to police a ceasefire, but to enforce the solution that provides security for both populations."[7] Before Iraq, Ignatieff thus advocated a "coalition of the willing" to invade the occupied territories and to liberate Palestinians from their apartheid-like oppression.

Perhaps it was an unconscious nod to Yasser Arafat's disastrous decision to endorse Saddam Hussein's "linking" of Iraqi withdrawal from Kuwait with an Israeli pullout from the occupied territories. Like Arafat after the 1991 Gulf War, after the 2003 invasion of Iraq Ignatieff rarely drew attention to this linkage again. Although his call for US troops on the Green Line is mentioned in *Empire Lite*, it's by then moot because he has clearly hitched his "humanitarian" wagon to the imperial horse. And on this ride, sadly for the Palestinians and their like around the world, "modern imperial ethics can only be hypocritical" (EL, p. 94).

When Ignatieff came back to Canada brandishing his ambition for the top office in the land, hypocrisy on matters Middle Eastern was a requisite. As a rookie Member of Parliament, he learned the hard way that these double standards would have to be maintained in a disciplined fashion. This lesson came about in the context of Israel's 2006 bombardment and invasion of Lebanon, aimed at crushing the forces of Hezbollah. Over 1,000 people were killed, the vast majority Lebanese, and the attack displaced over one million people, mostly in southern Lebanon. Israel's disproportionate violence shocked world public opinion, and mobilized Canada's large Lebanese community, which included many dual citizens living in Lebanon and trying to flee the violence. Nonetheless, Conservative Prime Minister Harper held the line for Israel, calling their actions "measured." Harper's tune did not change, even when Israel bombed a UN observation post, killing a UN peacekeeper.

On July 30, 2006, Israeli air strikes destroyed a three-story building in the village of Qana in southern Lebanon. Twenty-eight civilians were killed instantly, including 16 children. In an interview with the *Toronto Star*, Ignatieff described the massacre as "inevitable": "This is the kind of dirty war you're in when you have to do this and I'm not losing sleep about that."[8]

More than two months later, just weeks before the convention where he was bidding for leadership, Ignatieff appeared on a popular Quebec television talk-show.[9] Before his audience in this Canadian province which consistently polls the highest rates of support for the Arab position in the Middle East conflict, he said that he regretted the earlier remark:

> It was a mistake. I showed a lack of compassion. It was a mistake and when you make a mistake like that, you have to admit it. I was a professor of human rights, and I am also a professor of the laws of war, and what happened in Qana was a war crime, and I should have said that. That's clear.

The two statements do not, formally speaking, contradict each other. After all, if Ignatieff lost sleep over every war crime committed in wars he has supported, he would be a chronic insomniac. What he was really attempting to atone for was the insensitivity of the remark about Qana. Nonetheless, the reaction to the perceived flip-flop by supporters of Israel was swift. Frank Dimant, B'nai Brith Canada's executive vice-president, objected to the "appalling" comment: "To call it a war crime is totally, totally unacceptable." Others voted with their feet. Susan Kadis, a Liberal MP and co-chair of Ignatieff's leadership campaign in Toronto, withdrew her support, saying, "Michael is an intelligent person and I would think that he would have a better handle on the Middle East." Old friend and leadership foe Bob Rae accused him of "flip-flopping three times in one week" and taunted, "I actually don't know where you stand on this issue."[10] From the other side, for many progressives the Lebanon War incident was another example of a characteristic identified by journalist Linda McQuaig: "Ignatieff seems to lack convictions, let alone basic human feeling."[11] Ignatieff's mishandling of this file, arguably, contributed to his losing the Liberal leadership vote later in 2006 to Stéphane Dion.

Fast-forward to January 2009, when Israel was in the midst of the devastating assault on Gaza. For three weeks, the 1.5 million Palestinians confined to this densely populated strip of land between southern Israel and Egypt were collectively punished on the pretext of dealing a blow to Hamas terrorists. Over 1300 Palestinians died; in contrast, Israel suffered only 13 deaths—a ratio of killing of 100 to 1.

Now Liberal leader, having just secured Dion's early ouster and the capitulation of his other rivals a month earlier, Ignatieff proceeded with extreme caution in his public comments on the situation in Gaza. Despite widespread global outrage at Israel's actions—condemnations and calls for ceasefire, unprecedented solidarity demonstrations in many cities globally—Ignatieff's limited comments on the Israeli massacres carefully echoed the pro-Israel views of Canada's governing Conservatives. Canadian Arab and Muslim communities—whose official leaderships tend to be in the Liberal fold—were vocally upset, but this time Ignatieff held the line for Israel:

> The Liberal Party of Canada unequivocally condemns the rocket attacks launched by Hamas against Israeli civilians and calls for an immediate end to these attacks. We affirm Israel's right to defend itself against such attacks, and also its right to exist in peace and security.[17]

This official statement, although it included a pro forma call for a ceasefire and two-state solution, amounted to a blank check for Israel. The formulation reiterates the lie that it was Hamas who broke the ceasefire rather than Israel; implies that the latter is acting only in self-defense; and calls for an end to rocket attacks from Gaza without making a similar demand with regard to the exponentially more violent and deadly attack on Gaza by Israel.

Ignatieff preemptively defended Israel (and himself) in the

event of Qana-style massacres: "Hamas is a terrorist organization and Canada can't touch Hamas with a 10-foot pole. Hamas
is to blame for organizing and instigating these rocket attacks and
then for sheltering among civilian populations."[13] The discipline
Ignatieff showed this time around was preceded by another twist
in the saga of his 2006 comments about Qana. Adding another flip
to his flop, Ignatieff appeared at the Holy Blossom Temple in 2008
to make amends for calling a war crime a war crime. He described
that incident as "the most painful experience of my short political
career, and it was an error."[14] In his remarks he went on to burnish
his close relationship with the "liberal Zionist" Isaiah Berlin as
evidence of his fealty for Israel.

It was in this context that my own activist engagements brought
me into contact with Ignatieff. His approval of Israel's three-week
long assault on the people of Gaza was the reason a small group
of us had gathered to picket Ignatieff's speaking engagement at
a downtown Vancouver pub in mid-January 2009. To Ignatieff's
credit, he agreed to take a question or two from us, provided we
then let him walk in the front door.

Despite the hastily organized nature of our protest, we nevertheless managed to greet the Liberal leader with some creative
chants—"Hey Mike, hey Mike, there's no such thing as Empire
Lite"—as he stepped out of his vehicle. Ignatieff and wife Suzanna
stopped in front of the pub, surrounded by our rag-tag group and
some nervous Liberal organizers. One of us threw Ignatieff a question about the hypocrisy of the one-sided nature of his statements
on Gaza. I confess I can't remember much of the answer, just
that its prologue was, as always, autobiographical: "I've traveled
to Palestine ... Hebron, Ramallah ..." When he finally paused, I
confronted him with a specific question:

"Mr. Ignatieff, numerous human rights group have condemned
Israel's January 6 bombing of the UN-run school in which as many
as 40 Palestinians were killed. Why have you not condemned this as
a war crime?" He hesitated, as if considering an answer. Impatient,
I added a follow-up. "Are you losing any sleep this time?" That was

his cue. Taking it, he put his head down and went inside. We continued with our chanting for a while, adding a little background
noise to the drinking and networking inside the pub. But on this
night, it was the silence that mattered. Michael Ignatieff proved he
had learned a lesson that still holds sway over so much of official
politics in the western world.

Don't talk about Palestine.

# 6 STAYING THE COURSE IN AFGHANISTAN

*In their deluded efforts to be seen as global statesmen, Ignatieff and his foreign affairs critic, Bob Rae, managed to remove the Afghan albatross from around Harper's neck by volunteering to have Canadian soldiers stay at war for another three years. Harper can thank his stars. With enemies like the Liberals, who needs friends?*
—Thomas Walkom[1]

*Imperialism used to be the white man's burden. This gave it a bad reputation. But imperialism doesn't stop being necessary just because it becomes politically incorrect.*—Michael Ignatieff, *Empire Lite*

No mea culpa was ever forthcoming from Michael Ignatieff with respect to the war in Afghanistan. On the contrary, since returning to Canadian politics, he has consistently assisted the minority Conservative government in extending Canada's role in the military occupation. In fact, when it looked like Harper might have finally been ready to bow to public opinion and definitively pull out of Afghanistan, Ignatieff seized the country by the scruff of the neck and demanded we keep up our responsibilities to empire.

Ignatieff's practical impact on Canadian politics has arguably been greatest with respect to the war in Afghanistan, Canada's longest and most significant military intervention since the Korean War. Characteristically, Ignatieff made his case for "staying the course" in the conflict by deploying his own CV—*j'y étais, alors je sais.*

In *The Warrior's Honour*, Ignatieff gave an eyewitness account of the Taliban's first weeks of control of the Afghan capital, Kabul, in fall 1996. Arriving in the "Dresden of post–Cold War conflict" on an aid flight from Peshawar, Ignatieff toured the devastated city, mostly interviewing the beleaguered Red Cross workers and officials. At the Intercontinental Hotel, he even interviewed Taliban soldiers, the new rulers of the country. Ignatieff gave an accurate summary of the country and its warrior traditions:

> The Afghans are a border people, on the spiny buffer between civilizations—Iran, India, Central Asia—and have fought everyone from Alexander to the British army to keep a stubborn independence alive. They have a reputation as being among the most redoubtable guerrillas of all time. Their tradition of fighting— based on small, mobile units that avoid direct attack or pitched battle, seeking instead to use the mountain passes to ambush the enemy and surround it—was what brought them victory against the Russians. It was a tradition that respected the ecology of a poor society and the climate of a mountainous one: war began once the crop was planted or the animals were put up in the pastures, and it stopped when the harvest came and the snows descended. War was endemic, but it was self-limiting. (WH, p.144)

Ignatieff also described how, after the Soviet withdrawal, the country had descended into a brutal war, as "the weapons left behind by the Russians, and those shipped in by the Americans—from tanks to Stinger missiles—were so powerful that they overwhelmed the self-limiting ecology of warrior traditions." He failed to extend from this observation an explanation of the Taliban ascendancy in 1996. The Taliban, emerging in the early 1990s in the southern province of Kandahar to take over the majority of the country in a few short years, benefited from the support and backing of Pakistan and its intelligence service, the ISI. Historians and analysts of the region dispute whether and to what extent the United

States backed this development, or whether they were agnostic on the matter. But at the time there were certainly no anti-Taliban drums of war beating in Washington or other NATO capitals.

Perhaps this explains Ignatieff's rather ambivalent conclusions about Afghanistan. Back in 1996, he signed off from Kabul with those ruminations, cited above, about the Faustian bargain of war. Should the west take a relatively hands off approach and assist the victor in a civil war "to establish and sustain the monopoly of violence upon which order depends"? Or, should they "intervene on the side that appears to be most in the right and assist it to consolidate power"? The latter, according to Ignatieff, meant "accepting a moral pact with the devil of war, seeking to use its flames to burn a path to peace." As everyone knows, nothing burns a path to peace like a war stoked by the fires of Hell.

What could logically explain Ignatieff's indecisiveness, after eye-witnessing the first days of the Taliban's retrograde, misogynist rule over Afghanistan? The answer of course is that Ignatieff takes his war-cry cues from others, and in Afghanistan none were as yet forthcoming. Instead, the United States and other NATO partners were pursuing the normal options, quite distinct from the false, altruistic dichotomy of choices presented by Ignatieff. The US and its proxies continued to provide some material and logistical support to the so-called Northern Alliance of warlords who held on to small pockets of Afghanistan and engaged in mostly low intensity fighting with the Taliban. At the same time, US government and corporate interests engaged diplomatically with the Taliban, exploring how the regime might be beneficial to their interests. One highlight of this courtship occurred in the Texas of then-governor George W. Bush in 1997, when a Taliban delegation was put up in a luxury hotel and otherwise wined and dined—with "halal meat and Coca-Cola," according to press reports—by executives of the US energy giant Unocal, which hoped to secure a contract for a pipeline from Turkmenistan across Afghanistan.[2]

A little over five years later, Ignatieff returned to Afghanistan soon after the fall 2001 US invasion that followed the 9/11 terrorist attacks on New York and Washington. This time around, he was much more assertive about the need for imperial military intervention, presumably in support of the side "most in the right." He described his trip in *Empire Lite*, his 2003 book calling for heavy empire building in the world's "frontier zones."

He begins the chapter "Nation-building lite" with a description of the scene outside a fortified compound in the northern city of Mazar-e-Sharif, where two of the most powerful warlords in northern Afghanistan are trying to work out a deal. Ignatieff sets the scene:

> The bulky American in combat camouflage, multi-pocket waist-coat, wraparound sunglasses and floppy fishing hat is not going to talk to me. He may be CIA or Special Forces, but either way, I'm not going to find out. These people don't talk to reporters. But in Mazar-e-Sharif, second city of Afghanistan, in this warlords' compound, with a Lexus and an Audi purring in the driveway, armed mujahedin milling by the gate and musclemen standing guard in tight black T-shirts and flak jackets and sporting the latest semi-automatic weapons, the heavy-set American is the one who matters. He comes with a team that includes a forward air controller who can call in air strikes from the big planes doing Daytona 500 loops high in the sky. No one knows how many CIA and Special Forces there are in the country—perhaps as few as 350 all told—but with uplinks to air power and precision weapons, who needs regiments of ground troops? (EL, p. 65)

Fellow Canadian writer Michael Neumann has likened passages like these "boots-on-the ground descriptions" to "Car and Driver puff pieces," noting Ignatieff's almost obsessive attention to the make and model of motor vehicles in war zones.[3] Even the metaphor for the US planes circling overhead is a reference to Nascar's most famous race—proof of his fast transition, the use of such a Middle Americanism as literary device would have been unimaginable during his London years.

More than the motor vehicles themselves, this opening passage establishes that it is the American who matters. The throwaway line about not needing ground troops is misdirection from Ignatieff's real thesis: namely, that the US needed to take its imperial mission more seriously. He warns: "If [the United States] won't sustain and increase its military presence here, the other internationals will start heading for the exit" (EL, p. 90). The real reason that the US presence was still "lite" in the early years of the Afghan occupation, as Ignatieff should have known, had to do with the necessary hypocrisy of the empire he celebrated. Donald Rumsfeld, then US Secretary of Defense, had insisted on maintaining a minimal number of ground troops, in part because the US was determinedly driving for war against Iraq.

Ignatieff only nods in the direction of these political considerations; he seems far more interested in pounding home the message to the meek war-makers in Washington: "Empires don't come lite. They come heavy, or they do not last. And neither does the peace they are meant to preserve" (EL, p. 67).

Afghanistan, of all places, might have clued Ignatieff in to the false premises of his assertion that sometimes the empire must choose the lesser of two evils. The first problem with this is the notion that a lesser evil can definitively be ascertained. Further, there is the fact that the situation in Afghanistan is not a simple two-sided civil war; it involves a complex, multi-ethnic jockeying for control between strongmen and their militias. Take Dostum, for example—as the United States did. Like the other senior warlords in Afghanistan who made up the Northern Alliance, Dostum's loyalty to the United States was bought with bags of cash from the CIA. It was the Northern Alliance that, in the fall of 2001, was allowed to take Kabul with ground troops while the United States bombed from the sky.

But this disparate Afghan coalition of the willing on the ground was tenuous and temporary. The major concern of the warlords, in reality, was the maintenance of their own private regional fiefdoms. Dostum has carved his out of northern Afghanistan through decades of brutality and opportunistic side-switching, and playing to the ethnic nationalism (chauvinism) of his Uzbek constituency. Through much of the Soviet occupation, he sided with the Russian invaders. His many war crimes, documented by Human Rights Watch among others, are infamous in Afghanistan.[4]

Despite this grisly record, Hamid Karzai appointed Dostum to the post of head of the Armed Forces. The position was largely symbolic—the Afghan National Army was, and remains, a disorganized and mostly impotent puppet fighting force—since the real power rests with the occupiers and with the private militias or the warlords. But Dostum's inclusion—along with a host of other known war criminals—was a clear indication that crude power negotiations would trump concerns for human rights, democracy, and women's rights. It was this Faustian bargain between the US and the warlords of Afghanistan which prompted a then 25-year-old Malalai Joya to risk her life at the 2003 Constitutional Assembly in Kabul. The youngest delegate in attendance, Joya was also the only one with the temerity to call things by their right names. Her brief speech made her a household name in Afghanistan, and briefly made headlines around the world.

If the likes of Ignatieff had paid serious attention to Joya, they would have better understood that the continued empowerment of men like General Dostum offers a key explanation for NATO's utter failure to win hearts and minds in Afghanistan. These warlords—most of them as brutally repressive as, or even worse than, the Taliban, many of them equally fundamentalist and anti-women in their outlook—had in fact already been badly discredited in the eyes of the Afghan people. Following the Soviet withdrawal of 1989, it was they who plunged the country into a savage civil war. The various factions shelled each other and reduced large sections of Kabul to rubble, killing over 80,000 people and wreaking more destruction on the capital than even the Soviets, while exchanging massacres throughout the country. Arguably, one of the reasons for the Taliban's rapid sweep into power during the years 1994–96 was that many Afghans viewed them as a potential lesser evil to the marauding warlords. A comparable dynamic continues to play itself out in many parts of Afghanistan today.

Not least in this regard is the province of Kandahar, in Afghanistan's Pashtun southeast, the birthplace of both the Taliban and the Karzai family.[5] It was to this most volatile region of occupied Afghanistan that Canadian troops were transferred in 2005 by then Liberal Prime Minister Paul Martin. The Canadian contingent, just under 3,000 troops, has suffered a higher rate of casualties than most other NATO partners, with a death toll now over 150.

In *Empire Lite*, Ignatieff offers a glimpse of one of the fundamental problems with the western military presence in Kandahar: "the essential contradiction in American efforts to stabilize Afghanistan is that in the south, at least, winning the war on terrorism means consolidating the power of the very warlords who are the chief obstacle to state-building" (EL, p. 73). Ignatieff does not name any warlords, and fails to pursue this point further. Readers are left to assume that a "heavier" US war effort would make these contradictions go away.

Much of the Canadian and international press was equally unmotivated to pursue this line of investigation, preferring maudlin odes to the valor of the troops and recycled NATO talking points—staples of the embedded war journalism of our times. Those who did follow the money, the guns, and the drugs in Kandahar found that all roads led to none other than President Karzai's brother, Ahmed Wali Karzai, who served as both governor and an Al Capone figure in the province. He became such an embarrassment to his sponsors in Washington that US officials leaked to the *New York Times* the fact that he had been on the CIA payroll for years.

> Ahmed Wali Karzai, the brother of the Afghan president and a suspected player in the country's booming illegal opium trade, gets regular payments from the Central Intelligence Agency, and has for much of the past eight years, according to current and former

American officials. The agency pays Mr. Karzai for a variety of services, including helping to recruit an Afghan paramilitary force that operates at the C.I.A.'s direction in and around the southern city of Kandahar, Mr. Karzai's home.[6]

Over the years, the allegations against Wali Karzai grew louder, and the generally fraudulent, corrupt, and nepotistic character of the Karzai regime became increasingly obvious to observers throughout the world. Nevertheless, ruling circles in Canada remained committed to the "Afghan mission." The Canadian war effort proved their fealty to the US Empire, allowed them to push for their stake in Afghanistan's recently revealed mineral riches,[7] and generally contributed to the militarization of society and popular culture. In many ways, Ignatieff seemed out of sorts in Canadian politics. But on this file he could feel right at home. Afghanistan allowed him to move beyond the embarrassing episode on Iraq and torture, and again take up the cause of war and empire. Together with Harper, they would seize the dozing dog of war-averse public opinion, making Canada bark again on the world stage.

While Ignatieff's position on Iraq clearly played a role in his initial defeat for the gig as Liberal leader, his hawkish stance on Afghanistan ruffled some feathers in the Liberal Party but jibed perfectly with the relatively united position of the Canadian elite.

## A HANDSHAKE SEALS THE PRO-WAR DEAL

Stephen Harper wasted little time in using the war to drive a wedge into the opposition.

On May 17, 2006, Captain Nichola Goddard was killed in Afghanistan, becoming Canada's first female casualty in combat since World War II. On the same day, in Ottawa, Harper narrowly won a vote to extend Canada's participation in the war by two more years, until 2009. The pro-war motion passed 149 to 145, with the help of a small group of opposition Liberal MPs. The most prominent and the most outspoken among them was Michael Ignatieff. He expressed his "unequivocal support for the mission" and urged

Canada to shift away from the "peace-keeping paradigm." After the vote, the prime minister walked across the aisle and shook Ignatieff's hand. In the wake of his unpopular vote with Harper, Ignatieff lectured Liberal supporters about the need to cast aside old illusions: "the thing that Canadians have to understand about Afghanistan is that we are well past the era of Pearsonian peace-keeping."[8] All this coming before his "mea culpa" on Iraq, it no doubt reinforced the fears of some Liberals and contributed to his narrowly losing the 2006 leadership vote.

Stéphane Dion voted against the 2006 extension of the war. A weak leader and poor communicator, he was never able or truly willing to bring the party to a unified position against extending the war. Appointing Ignatieff as deputy leader left him further hamstrung, and stuck with the war.

In February 2008, celebrating two years as prime minister, Harper announced that the government would introduce a confidence motion to put off the Afghan withdrawal another two years. If the vote had been defeated it would have sparked an election. Dion talked tough about being firm on withdrawal, but could not proceed to an election on the issue. I was told by a Liberal insider that Dion believed Afghanistan could be a winning election issue, but the internal opposition of both Ignatieff and Bob Rae stayed his hand. Eventually, Harper threw Dion a bone by adding language about "shifting focus" to "reconstruction and training," as well as promising a "hard end date" of 2011.[9]

For the next couple of years, the prime minister bent the rhetorical stick in order to prevent Afghanistan from gaining traction as an issue in electoral politics. He repeatedly insisted that Canadian troops would withdraw once and for all from Afghanistan in 2011. One startling example came in a March 2009 interview on CNN, with Harper explaining that his "own judgment is quite frankly we are not going to ever defeat the insurgency."

As public opinion grew increasingly against the war, another extension seemed improbable. But as the Obama administration sent in tens of thousands of additional troops throughout 2010, they turned up the heat on their NATO partners to provide a patina of multilateralism and share the military burden. On an official visit in early 2010, Hillary Clinton publicly urged Canada to reconsider its withdrawal, or at least find other ways to help the war effort.

Defense Minister Peter MacKay floated some trial balloons about keeping troops in Afghanistan as trainers, but each time the issue came up Harper insisted the military mission was winding down. Harking back to his *Empire Lite* days, Ignatieff stepped up to harangue those who would try to wage imperial occupation "on the cheap"; the Canadian people had to be reminded that empire and war "come heavy, or not at all."

## ONCE MORE UNTO THE BREACH WITH HARPER

In June 2010, Ignatieff spoke at Toronto's historic Royal York Hotel to a gathering of something called the "National Forum," a joint effort of the Canadian Club and the Empire Club, two century-old speakers' fora that boast members from among the "most influential leaders from the professions, business, labour, education and government."[10] Ignatieff was continuing a family tradition. His father George Ignatieff, a top Canadian diplomat, addressed the Empire Club in 1969;[11] his grandfather, Count Nicholas Ignatieff, the czarist minister who brought the family to Canada (via Britain) following the Bolshevik Revolution, spoke at 100 Front Street way back in 1938.[12]

George Ignatieff's memoir was entitled "The Making of a Peacemonger," and in 1969 the topic of his speech was "Canada's Stake in Arms Control and Disarmament." Michael was at the Royal York to boost war, to explain to the Empire Club why Canada should continue its commitment to the NATO occupation of Afghanistan. More than that, it was a reaffirmation of his core belief in liberal internationalism (read: interventionism), which Ignatieff asserted was one of the three core "simple things" foundational to the Liberal Party. The speech was a gift to Stephen Harper, who was aiming to extend Canada's military presence in Afghanistan but did not want the war to become an election issue. The speech simultaneously put Ignatieff and the Liberals out in front of Harper on the war (right where he wanted them) and allowed Ignatieff to once again openly advocate for a "liberal" imperialism that doesn't try to duck out of its heavy responsibilities.

In the speech, we can see both a certain incoherence and a hint of an awareness that the public might be wearying of the war:

Let's also remember what our goal in Afghanistan is. However strange as it may seem to say it, our goal in Afghanistan is peace too. This is a country I know well. I began to visit it first in 1997. I've seen it ravaged by civil war. I've seen the ethnic hatreds, the hatreds that have left millions dead. It's a tormented country. It became a haven for terror. We went in for good reason, to protect the national security of Canada. One hundred and forty seven brave Canadians didn't come home. This is on our conscience, this is on our hearts.

Mr. Harper behaves as if the Afghan mission never happened. It happened on his watch. He's walking away from it as if it never occurred. There's something about this that doesn't seem right to Canadians. We have to have an honest national discussion about where we go from here. We came in with an alliance, we came in to help an Afghan government. Canadians are serious people, if you ask us to do something serious and difficult we'll do it, provided Canadians can be convinced as to what it is we're trying to achieve. And the problem in my view has not been casualties, the problem has been futility, the sense of "what are we achieving, what progress are we making?" I'm very concerned that once the combat mission ends, and I believe the combat mission should end, and should end completely in 2011, we will walk away with the job undone. And we will look back and ask, "What was that about? Did we let ourselves down? Did we let our allies down? Did we let Afghanistan down?"

I think there is a place for Canada to commit to a training role, to train the military, to train the police. What were we there for in the beginning? It was to enable the Afghans to defend themselves. It's not our country, it's their country. The whole purpose of our engagement in that country was to enable that country to stand on its own feet and be self-sufficient. We're not yet there. Are Canadians content to walk away with the job half done? I think not. However difficult it may be to say so, I think there is more work to be done. A training mission focused on raising the capability of the officer cadre in Afghanistan is a mission we can do. It does not involve combat, but it involves building capacity. Remember peace, order and good government. We've got to build the capacity of this people so that they can defend themselves and so that we can come home with honour, with a sense Canadians always want to have, of a job well done, a difficult job well done.

And so we are open as a party to a national discussion about this: a serious, thoughtful, to the roots national discussion about what we can do. This is what parliament should do; this is what Canadians should do. You can't have a foreign policy unless it's based on a national conversation. Mr. Harper wants to stop that conversation, I want to start it.[13]

Although it may appear that Ignatieff had significantly toned down his pro-war politics, in fact he had recalibrated his rhetoric to the Canadian context. He was taking the initiative, outdoing Harper on support for the Afghan intervention. Beneath the assurances of working for peace, there is a strong subtext that the real problem has been Harper's lack of resolve and commitment to the war effort. In effect, Ignatieff is accusing the Conservative government of pretending to wind down the war when they know full well that Canada's establishment remains committed to helping the counter-insurgency, and to maintaining the occupation.

In November 2010, the predictable endgame played out, in the week leading up to a major NATO summit in Portugal. One day, seemingly *ex nihilo*, Harper announced that a contingent of up to 1,000 Canadian staff and troops would remain in Afghanistan after 2011, to "train" the Afghan army and police forces. After making some vague noises about wanting to see "a plan" from

Harper, Ignatieff and the Liberals allowed the extension to take place without even a vote in the House of Commons. Some Liberal MPs were quoted anonymously expressing their unhappiness with both Rae and Ignatieff. A vote in the House might have exposed these party divisions, so Ignatieff was only too happy to let Harper get away with it.

Political pundit Chantal Hébert explains how Ignatieff, and his foreign affairs shadow minister Bob Rae, painted themselves into a corner:

> they have jointly managed the singular achievement of giving Harper the elbow room he needed to change tack on Afghanistan in a way that is bound to please both NATO and the Conservative party base while making the Liberals more vulnerable to Bloc Québécois and NDP attacks on both Afghanistan and parliamentary accountability in the next election.[14]

Would that it were so. Since the end of 2008, the social democrats had been dozing next to the fires of war, seduced and sedated by the "Obama effect." Like their counterparts on the liberal Left in the United States, their opposition to the war had been muted. Swept up in cross-border euphoria, NDP politicians and communications professionals tried to import Obamamania into Canada. In 2008, NDP leader Jack Layton sprinkled some references to "hope" and "change" into his speeches. The 2009 NDP convention in Halifax featured multiple former Obama advisors or campaign workers as keynote speakers. An even further abasement was made evident in discussions about a possible name-change for the NDP, dropping the "New" to become a north-of-the-border "Democratic Party."

More damaging was what the NDP leadership excised from their public utterances. Through 2009 and 2010, the demand for bringing the troops home was only mentioned in the most *pro forma* manner (it was given one line in Layton's official 2009 speech to convention). Even before Obama had won his election, Afghanistan was barely raised by the NDP during the 2008

Canadian election campaign. And so it was that Canada became set to stay the course in Afghanistan until 2014 and perhaps beyond. Back at their 2006 convention, the NDP had promised to unite with the anti-war movement to push for an end to the occupation. The keynote speaker at that party gathering had been Malalai Joya. Her words should ring loudly in the ears of Layton and his handlers: "The silence of the good people is worse than the actions of the bad."

# 7 THE LAST INVASION

*I made a very conscious decision to go from being a watcher at the pond, or a man at the hockey rink, up in the blues, to being on the ice. And I knew the minute I did it I was no longer a journalist. I was no longer a spectator, I was an actor.* —Michael Ignatieff[1]

## MEA (SORTA) CULPA

Due in no small part to his record on Iraq and torture, and to his awkward flip-flopping on Israel-Palestine, Michael Ignatieff went down to defeat in his bid for the Liberal leadership at the party's convention in August 2006.

Almost exactly one year later, and with another leadership bid in mind, Ignatieff finally conceded publicly his mistake on Iraq. Even though he was by then established as a Canadian politician, he chose to file his pseudo-apology back at the scene of his crime, in the *New York Times Magazine*. "Long on *mea*, short on *culpa*," as Canadian journalist Linda McQuaig succinctly described it, Ignatieff's confession of wrongdoing left much to be desired, and raised more questions about his judgment and politics than it answered.[2]

His essay, "Getting Iraq Wrong," starts by admitting that "the unfolding catastrophe in Iraq" had condemned the judgment of both the president and of intellectual fellow travelers like himself.[3] He lamented the now "distant dream" of a free Iraq of which an

"Iraqi exile friend" had told him the night the war started. The friend in question was the aforementioned Kanan Makiya, a neighbor of Ignatieff's in Cambridge, and one of a number of ex-Trotskyists who had become ideologues of the neo-conservative movement. In January 2003, Makiya was quoted in the *New York Times* extolling President Bush's "intense commitment to a genuinely democratic post-Saddam Iraq."[4] It's not clear why Ignatieff would reference one of the few intellectuals even more discredited than he was by the Iraqi quagmire, unless it was a matter of trying to pass the buck. In that case he should have mentioned Makiya by name.

Plenty of other names are dropped into the piece, starting with Isaiah Berlin, and followed by Roosevelt, Churchill, De Gaulle, Bismarck, Samuel Beckett, and (Bob Rae's favorite) Edmund Burke, among others. It's as if Ignatieff is lining up star witnesses in his defense, even though he's purportedly entering a guilty plea. By the end, he winds up raising other, new suspicions about his character and judgment, at the very least.

To Berlin he attributes the observation that "the trouble with academics and commentators is that they care more about whether ideas are interesting than whether they are true." In contrast, Ignatieff asserts, politicians "can't afford the luxury" of considering ideas merely for their own sake. At first glance a banal truth, this is actually a case of self-serving misdirection. Ignatieff expands the false dichotomy, stating that "good judgment in political life looks different than good judgment in intellectual life." Unlike the intellectual, we are told, the politician "must not confuse the world as it is with the world as they wish it to be."

As McQuaig points out, "This notion that 'useless' ideas—such as voicing support for an upcoming military invasion—can be harmlessly entertained inside the academic world, would be worrisome enough if students were the only ones subjected to the ideas."[5]

If his article's windy preamble has any purpose at all, it is to distract from the reason Ignatieff is having to apologize in the first place. His judgments on Iraq did matter, just as much as the politicians' judgments mattered, because he was in a position of great influence when he expounded his views in favor of the war. In mistakenly supporting the war he was, in fact, relatively rare among academics and intellectuals; taken globally, outside of the politically backward halls of American academia, his position was an outlier, exceedingly rare and held in disdain by the majority of his colleagues. In contrast, the overwhelming majority of American politicians got Iraq wrong. And this is partly why his views were so sought after. He had the ear of power, just like Makiya, because power desperately needed the window-dressing intellectuals like him provided for their empire-building plans.

Implicit in Ignatieff's pseudo-apology is a message: "Don't worry," he seems to say, "I'm a politician now, so you can trust that I won't let myself get carried away with ideas." But the essay, of course, is a continuation of his life as a public intellectual—there is no real demarcation. The piece is over-stocked with plenty of rhetoric about what makes "great politicians," how they learn to make sound decisions and leave good impressions with the electorate. He seems to be, at least subconsciously, explaining away his failure as an intellectual with assurances that he understands his new role as a politician—though perhaps this is giving Ignatieff too much credit. To be perfectly, and vulgarly, blunt, when you've read as much of his writing as I have, it's hard not to be left with the impression that Ignatieff is a man simply incapable of turning off the flow of bullshit. Whether concluding an entire book about his Russian ancestors with a throw-away line about their remoteness and relative unimportance to even *his own* life, or adding endless, labyrinthine prevarications and caveats to the majority of porcelain-delicate assertions he does make, Ignatieff leaves his audience with nothing if not the impression that he will say anything that comes to mind to fill a void otherwise left to either silence or someone else's thoughts.

Regardless, Ignatieff's reflections on the good political life are, really, neither here nor there with respect to the issue about which he is ostensibly writing—Iraq. Referring to Bush in his essay, he writes:

> The sense of reality that might have saved him from catastrophe would have taken the form of some warning bell sounding inside, alerting him that he did not know what he was doing. But then, it is doubtful that warning bells had ever sounded in him before. He had led a charmed life, and in charmed lives warning bells do not sound.

Writing about Bush, he could easily be describing his own "charmed life." But this pop psychology explanation is just wrong on myriad levels. The worst thing about it is that it elides the rational strategic calculations that led the imperial power to its relentless drive for war in the first place. Unlike Bush, Ignatieff did not have the excuse of not knowing the difference between Sunni, Shia, and Kurd, but that doesn't stop him from claiming that everyone had judged Iraq based on "faulty intelligence and lack of knowledge of Iraq's fissured sectarian history."

So, whence does reliable knowledge emanate? At the tender age of 60, Ignatieff finally discovers this shocking truth: "a sense of reality doesn't always flourish in elite institutions ... Bus drivers can display a shrewder grasp of what's what than Nobel Prize winners." Bus drivers! It turns out that bus drivers and many other subliterate proletarians had realized early on what it took the obtuse Ignatieff more than four years and countless war dead to figure out. But more than the clamoring of the bus drivers, perhaps it was the harsh wake-up call delivered by Liberal Party delegates at the 2006 leadership convention that had finally pushed Ignatieff to see "what's what" on Iraq.

Ignatieff adds one final, nauseating twist to his pseudo-apology, impugning the motives of those who had opposed the war: "many of those who correctly anticipated catastrophe did so not by exercising judgment but by indulging in ideology." Right after praising the shrewd assessments of reality made by bus drivers and their ilk, he accuses them of knee-jerk opposition based on conspiracy theories about Bush being "only after the oil." Ignatieff, of course, had earlier admitted that the war was about oil, practically begging his liberal American readership to get over the embarrassment in order just to embrace the geostrategic imperatives behind the war.

Ignatieff, it seemed, had learned little or nothing from Iraq. This did not bode well for the outcome of his final, hubris-fuelled invasion: the conquest of Canada.

In December 2008, the Liberal leadership fell suddenly to Ignatieff like a ripe fruit, seeming to confirm his manifest destiny to rule Canada. Following a dismal election campaign that fall, Stéphane Dion had announced that he would step down as Liberal leader. Then, in an unexpected and (for Canada) historic development, Dion and the NDP's Jack Layton reached an agreement to form a coalition, bolstered by a more limited partnership with the sovereigntist, mostly social democratic Bloc Québécois. After expressing non-confidence in Harper's minority Conservatives, the opposition coalition asked the Governor General—the Queen's representative in Canada—to allow them to form a government. This precipitated a full-blown political crisis in Canada, with government ministers making wild charges of a coup d'état to the international press. Ultimately, Governor General Michaëlle Jean acceded to Harper's request to prorogue parliament for two months, which would allow him to buy the necessary time to kill the coalition's momentum. Many of the more conservative elements in the Liberal Party had never wanted any part of the coalition with "socialists and separatists"—as Harper's Conservatives relentlessly branded it—and Ignatieff became their champion. He had been the last member of the Liberal caucus to sign on to the coalition agreement, and, as Harper successfully moved public opinion against the project, prorogation gave the Liberals time to back out. They did this by having Ignatieff's declared rivals for the party leadership back out of the race. This included his closest competitor, Bob Rae, who would have to again play second fiddle to his evidently less qualified friend.

Almost from the first as party leader, Ignatieff received a cool reception in public opinion polls. This led him to speculate—in writing, of course—about how he could become a better politician. The (as ever) solipsistic nature of Ignatieff's pseudo-apology on Iraq became a sort of leitmotif for many of these ruminations about how he might achieve "greatness" in politics.

In early 2009, *The New Yorker* ran a mostly sympathetic piece about Michael Ignatieff's struggles as leader of the Liberal Party of Canada.[6] Written by a friendly acquaintance, Adam Gopnik, the article gives the intellectual-turned-politician plenty of space to explain himself. One scene takes place in the car, on the way to Stratford, Ontario, to watch a performance of Shakespeare's Macbeth (even the friendly Gopnik seems to allude to the relevance of the evening fare). Ignatieff reaches for a hockey analogy— Nascar references will no longer do much good—and comes up short: "The thing that politics most strongly resembles is being on soccer teams and hockey teams when I was a child. It's not a lonely writer in his den thinking thoughts. What is it that a great politician knows? What is that form of knowledge?" He mulls the question further and tells Gopnik of an experience he had not too long ago with his wife:

> Last night, Zsuzsanna and I were watching the Detroit Red Wings goalie, and he knows something; what is it that he knows? What is it that a great politician knows? The great ones have a skill that is just jaw-dropping, and I'm trying to learn that.

*The Detroit Red Wings goalie.* The elocution betrays his lack of familiarity with the sport of the Canadian masses. Furthermore, the inapt (and inept) comparison shows that Ignatieff just doesn't get why he doesn't get Canadian politics. *"What is it that [the hockey goaltender] just knows?"*

The athlete in question was Chris Osgoode, who was at the time enjoying a last hurrah of quality play at the end of a long, successful professional career. In fact, after a dismal regular season, he was in the midst of a brief few weeks of stellar play through the playoffs. As it happens, I know what Osgoode knows about being good at what he does. When Osgoode was a teenager, I watched him play goalie against the Kamloops Blazers in British Columbia's Western Hockey League, the rough and tumble antechamber to the professional leagues. As he faced down hard rubber coming at 80 miles per hour, thousands of rowdy, alcohol-fuelled fans in Kamloops would serenade the young player with chants of "Osgoode ... No good!"

Night after pressure-filled night, the young Osgoode mastered his profession, learning to turn away the rubber and tune out the relentless taunting. By 2009, in his late thirties, we're talking three decades of accumulated experience, routine, relentless practice and study of the game. No dilettante could drop in and pick up that "something" which Osgoode had acquired through long apprenticeship.

But for Ignatieff—to modify Ron Graham's phrasing in *The Walrus*—the question was not whether he could become a great politician, but how. Keeping to the sports analogies, it reminds me of reading about basketball legend Michael Jordan's doomed and much decided try-out as a professional baseball player. In discussing his struggles with journalist Bob Greene over the course of many months, Jordan never betrayed the slightest hint of doubt about his own abilities. It was simply a matter of finding the key to unlocking potential greatness. He was wrong—but unlike the other Michael, at least Jordan was only trying out for the minor league.

## A LIBERAL INTERPRETATION OF CANADIAN HISTORY

September 2008: It's a typical Liberal election rally, and deputy leader Michael Ignatieff has the microphone in front of a modest crowd gathered outside the party's office in Hamilton, Ontario. It's just another day on the campaign trail. Candidate and MP Ignatieff is in town—a short drive south from his own riding in Toronto—to boost the Liberals' three candidates in the area. In exhorting the Liberals' foot soldiers, he combines a recap of his youthful stint as a party activist with a fairly standard partisan interpretation of the Liberals' historic role in Canada.

> When I was 17 years old I knocked on doors for Mike Pearson. And I then worked on the campaign plane for Pierre Trudeau … Our party is not just a party. It's a national institution. And where the Liberal Party planted the stake, that was the centre of Canadian politics. We are not a party of the Left. We are a party of the centre. And where we planted the centre stake, that's where the centre was. And because we planted the stake there, Canada has medicare, Canada has the Canada Pension Plan, *nous habitons un pays bilingue, fière de l'être*, we support culture, we support the arts, we look after those who are less fortunate, we are the party of the Charter of Rights and Freedoms, everybody in this crowd, every person in this crowd can look every other person in this crowd and say "I'm a Canadian, I'm no better than you I'm not worse than you, I'm equal to you." That equality, that equality is the core of what we believe in. I tell you and I tell you without arrogance, I tell you with simple pride, we created the country you live in, never forget it.

Then, he concludes with a warning:

> And what Stephen Harper wants to do—they talk about his secret agenda but it's not a secret—is to replace the Liberal Party as the natural governing party of Canada. And if he succeeds he'll pick up that stake where we planted it in the middle of Canadian life, and he will move it 1, 2, 3, 4, 5, 6, 7, 8, 9, 10 degrees to the right … And I swear to you in a couple of mandates you won't recognize the country you live in.

This banal campaign speech epitomizes the Canadian version of "lesser evilism" in electoral politics. It can be understood using the three steps of a magic trick: the set-up (or the pledge), the turn, and the prestige. The pledge, wherein the Liberals are credited for the progressive policies that appeal to their audience's basic sense of fairness and equality, is crucial. This conceit makes the Conservatives' right-wing agenda all the more fearsome. At the same time, Ignatieff clearly defines the Liberals in the political center. The turn, in this case, is to invite the audience to imagine Harper destroying those elements of the welfare state they hold dear, further tearing up the social fabric, and to imply that the Liberals are the only thing holding him back. The prestige, the effect of the illusion, is to make the political Left—past, present, and future—disappear altogether.

This political sleight-of-hand is an old trick, par for the course for Liberal politicians. A cursory study of the real history of social gains toward equality in Canadian history shows Ignatieff's assertion that "we built this country" to be plainly false. On Medicare, and the whole notion of health care for all, the real pioneering was done by the democratic socialist provincial government in the province of Saskatchewan. Its implementation federally only came after many long, hard years of advocacy by the NDP opposition in Ottawa. The same is true of old-age pensions, which were a concession extracted from a minority Liberal government when the NDP held the balance of power.

This and much more social history of Canada is no longer common knowledge, especially among the younger generation. Like almost every other social democratic party in the western world, the NDP is a hollowed-out shell of its former self. It functions as an electoral machine, and only rarely functioning at all as a vehicle for serious issue-based campaigning, community organizing, or as a venue for political or popular education. As an electoral left alternative, the NDP has lost much of its edge. And when it does come out swinging, its positions are ignored or maligned in the corporate media. As Ignatieff himself observed, back in 2000: "I'm no Marxist, but I am astonished that social and economic inequality … has simply disappeared from the political agenda in Canada and most other capitalist societies. This disappearance has something to do with rights talk. It can capture civil and political inequalities, but it can't capture more basic economic inequalities" (RR, pp. 19–20).

It's not that the NDP under Jack Layton has undergone a complete Blairite conversion to neo-liberalism, but they do lack the temerity to run on even a mildly aggressive social democratic program. And, as discussed, they have failed for long stretches to take up the anti-war cause over Afghanistan. So, absent a clearly articulated social democratic (let alone socialist) alternative, and without any other visible source of progressive leadership, Ignatieff could well "pass" as a lesser evil. Certainly, there are some differences between Ignatieff and Harper over domestic policy, but then, Canadian domestic policy has never been Ignatieff's keenest interest.

After five years of Prime Minister Stephen Harper and two of Liberal leader Michael Ignatieff, it's true that in some respects Canadians no longer recognize their country. Some Liberals may no longer recognize their party. Take the issue of US war resisters, dozens of whom have fled to Canada over the past decade to avoid serving in the occupations of Afghanistan and Iraq. The vast majority are conscientious objectors to the illegal invasion of Iraq, and for years a grassroots campaign has sought to have the Canadian Parliament pass a clear resolution granting asylum to these resisters. Harper, in a show of fealty to the long-departed Bush administration, has stubbornly refused any steps in that direction. The NDP has always supported the resisters, but has been unable to pass any bills in the Commons. Finally, after tedious months and years of campaigning, the war resisters caught a break, as Liberal MP Gerard Kennedy stepped up to sponsor a private member's bill that would allow US war resisters sanctuary in Canada. For Ignatieff, it seemed like an issue he could now easily get behind, if only to bury the lingering distaste of his once ardent support for the Iraq War. On September 29, 2010, MPs stood to vote on the second reading of Bill C-440. Just before the vote was called, Michael Ignatieff and about a dozen other Liberal MPs walked out of the parliamentary chamber. The war resisters' right to stay in Canada was defeated 143 to 136. As on Afghanistan, the unofficial Harper-Ignatieff coalition carried the day.

On May 2, 2011, in what must surely amount to the most shocking election result to hit Canada in decades, Ignatieff's Liberal Party was reduced to a rump third party, plummeting from 77 to 34 seats in the House of Commons. Astonishingly, Ignatieff even lost his own riding in a formerly "safe" Liberal seat in suburban Toronto.

With the Liberal collapse, the Harper Conservatives finally won their long-coveted majority government. The Liberals were supplanted as the Official Opposition after an almost completely unforeseen surge by the NDP. The social democrats took over, winning more than 100 seats, including an astonishing 59 in Quebec.

The morning after the humiliation of election night, Ignatieff resigned. A golden parachute of sorts cushioned the fall, as within days it was announced he had accepted a teaching position at the University of Toronto. A week later Ignatieff showed up in Ottawa to say farewell to his Liberal colleagues and the Ottawa press corps, before jetting off for a vacation in France.

Why did Ignatieff fail to capture the imagination of Canadian voters? Sheer ignorance of the country he sought to govern is at least part of the explanation.

Near the end of Ignatieff's *True Patriot Love*—an exploration of the men in his mother's family, which was rushed to publication in an effort to assert his Canadian *bona fides*—we are treated to a play-by-play of the road trip he and his wife took in 2000, retracing the pioneering sea-to-sea journey of his great-grandfather.

George Monro Grant used his 1872 expedition as the basis for his book *Ocean to Ocean*, essentially a propaganda tract for the railway barons of the CPR. Ignatieff possibly hoped that the reminiscences of his summer vacation spent slumming it out west—he and his wife took the back roads, searched for homemade pie and "stayed in small motels where we shared hot tubs or pools with truckers with sunburnt arms and faces"—would help his electability.

But whatever populist points the travel diary might have scored were nullified once the couple reached Edmonton. Ignatieff writes: "We headed straight for West Edmonton Mall. My children had joined us by then and they had been told the mall was the largest in the world" (TPL, p. 163). Non-Canadian audiences may not fully appreciate this *faux pas*, something akin to an aspiring Chinese premier saying "My kids had heard it was one of the biggest walls in the world." A testament to the tacky consumerism of the 1980s, "West Ed"—with its indoor amusement park, waterslides, ice rink, and submarines—was equal parts beloved and notorious across Canada, a country whose every citizen knew it was, for a time at least, the biggest mall in the world. Ignatieff, though, was living abroad during the mall's entire 23-year reign as the world's largest, 1981–2004. Reading this section, I half expected Ignatieff to mention a statue of "some guy named Gretzky," especially given his past disparaging remarks about Ukrainians.

And Edmonton—or, as it's sometimes called in the Tory-blue world of Alberta politics, 'Redmonton'—is a city that a Liberal can't afford to alienate. The worldly Ignatieff, though, seems to have a very limited grasp of North American urban centers in general. On a western swing in 2009, while making a "whistle-stop" trip on the new airport-to-downtown train line in notoriously transit-deficient Vancouver, he stopped to tell two dumbstruck employees: "You're working in the best public transit system ... probably in North America, so you must feel very proud of it."[7]

Lacking anything resembling a Chrétien-like populist touch, Ignatieff's western strategy put a premium on full-scale pandering to the powerful oil industry. In the 2008 federal election, the carbon tax proponent Stéphane Dion and his Liberals were shut out of Alberta, and all but shut out of the west. Ignatieff desperately wanted to turn this around. He was so keen to win seats in Alberta, in fact, that he was willing to trash the planet and sabotage the fight against climate change in the process. At least, that's what his tar sands boosterism would seem to have indicated.

In early 2009, at an event in Vancouver, Ignatieff gave this response—substituting the industry-friendly term "oil sands"—to a young person's earnest question about what he planned to do about the tar sands:

> This is where a chill falls over the room because everybody expects me to say that they're terrible and we've got to shut them down. Absolutely not ... and for once the word "awesome," that we overuse all the time, is truly what you feel when you're there. It is awe-inspiring. The capital investment, the sheer size of this thing, the fact that there are 100 years of deposits ...[8]

Ignatieff was positively gushing, exhorting his young audience to understand "how powerful the oil sands make us." This sort of indulging in grandiose rhetoric about Alberta's tar sands was par for the course with Ignatieff. In July 2009, during the Stampede, he flattered a Calgary audience, "We have to be a party that understands that the beating heart of the Canadian economy, the beating heart of the future of our country, is in Alberta." Before that, he told the Edmonton Chamber of Commerce, "The West is where the destiny of our country's economy will be played out"[9]

As for those who have pointed out that the destiny of the world's climate crisis will be played out in no small part in northeastern Alberta, Ignatieff had no time. When *National Geographic* did a feature story on "The Canadian Oil Boom"[10] that included a shocking photo essay on the moonscapes and toxic "tailings ponds" it leaves in its wake, the Liberal leader declared, "I don't take lessons from National Geographic." A more noxious soundbyte emission would be hard to imagine. On this file, Ignatieff and Harper were in more or less perfect agreement. When it comes to his stance on Alberta's bitumen oil production, one almost longs for the Thatcher-era Ignatieff who "felt that Britain could not continue to produce so much coal."[11]

Predictably, none of this translated into any electoral gains in Alberta. The Liberals under Ignatieff were shut out of Alberta, and reduced to a mere five seats west of Ontario. The Liberal losses in Ontario and Quebec may not have been unrelated to his bombast about Canada's "economic destiny" out west; in addition to the negative environmental impacts of the western oil economy, there is also its inflation of the Canadian dollar, which has wreaked havoc on eastern manufacturing. There are, to be sure, Albertans who oppose the reckless development of the tar sands; the only non-Conservative MP in the province, the NDP's Linda Duncan, founded the Environmental Law Centre in Edmonton. She and NDP leader Jack Layton used their campaign plane to take the media on a fly-over of the tar sands on the first day of the 2008 federal election campaign.

During that campaign, a big effort was made by some to call for strategic voting—essentially an "anybody but Harper" tactic, urging a vote for the Liberal, NDP, or Bloc candidate (or Green leader Elizabeth May) deemed most likely to defeat their Tory opponent—through the voteforenvironment.ca website. Despite the Liberals' atrocious record on greenhouse gas emissions while in power, this call had a certain appeal, given the fact that Stéphane Dion had made the so-called "Green Shift" the centerpiece of his platform. (In a fit of earnestness, Dion even named his dog Kyoto.) Next time around, especially for those at all concerned about global warming and the environment, it was much harder to make the case that a vote for Ignatieff's Liberals was a strategic one.

Ignatieff's boosterism of the war in Afghanistan reaped similarly disastrous fruit for the Liberals. The only part of the country where Harper's Conservatives failed to make gains in the 2011 election was Quebec. Traditionally staunchly anti-war, Quebec never warmed to Ignatieff. *Toronto Star* columnist Chantal Hébert identified the Liberals' move to help extend the military presence in Afghanistan as the point where "Quebec lost interest in the Liberals."[12] The NDP, although quiet in recent years in their opposition to the Afghanistan mission, was viewed by Quebec as an acceptable alternative reflective of the widespread anti-war sentiment.

Ignatieff's last foreign policy adventure resulted in another quagmire. In the end, his dreams of conquest proved almost as delusional in Canada as they did in Iraq. His "opposition" allowed the Tories to govern the country for years essentially unopposed on many files, in the process tilting Canadian politics further to the right. Without a clear, dignified exit strategy, Ignatieff was doomed to watch helplessly as Harper's Conservatives won a majority government, coming close to fulfilling their ultimate aim of supplanting the Liberals as the "natural governing party" of Canada.

## CONCLUSION

In the early days of the 2011 federal election campaign, Michael Ignatieff sought to frame the contest as a two-way race—between the greater and the lesser evil, you could say—insisting that the choice for Canadians was between the "blue door (Conservative) and the red door (Liberal)." What this rather wooden metaphor elided was that both doors led to the same corporate boardrooms.

As it happened, voters chose to open another door, with the NDP surging into official opposition status with over 30 percent of the vote. Canada's social democratic party is something of an outlier among the liberal democracies. Unlike in the United States, it exists and has played an important role in shaping politics but, unlike in most of Europe, it has never held power at the federal level.

The millions of new votes for social democracy reflected neither an endorsement of the Blairite inclinations of much of the party's leadership nor a clear yearning for a strong anti-corporate alternative. But the vote did reflect the disaffection of an increasing number with politics as usual.

In fact, the NDP's election platform differed little from Ignatieff's. Both offered some very modest increases in social spending; both vowed not to carry out the latest corporate tax cuts, but otherwise neither seriously threatened to challenge any of the prerogatives of corporate Canada. Having spent much of his time in Canadian politics staking out a center-right position on key policies, Ignatieff ran the election campaign of a moderate social democrat. The result was that neither voters on the right nor on the left bought what Ignatieff was selling, opting instead for either Harper's hard-right conservatism or Jack Layton's warmed-over social democracy.

As elsewhere, liberals and social democrats have in many ways become indistinguishable. Or at least interchangeable, as in the UK, where the Liberal Democrats seamlessly transitioned from being something of an anti-war, third party alternative to a warmonger-ing, neo-liberal Labour government to playing coalition partner to a neo-warmongering, neo-liberal Conservative government.

The larger problem is not so much that the leaders of the NDP are latent betrayers or, more accurately, insufficiently ambitious reformers. The problem is that the Left as a whole lacks a coherent political program or vision. Had this not been the case, it would have been unimaginable that someone with Ignatieff's record could ever have even been taken half-seriously as a progressive or center-left alternative. Notwithstanding some promising new Left party initiatives in Europe, and the rise of the Left in Latin America, this problem is universal in our counter-revolutionary times. It is the central problem of the global Left today after the apparent death of the socialist alternative.

Among the more radical Left, the notion of a "politics of resist-ance" holds sway—the idea of fighting to attain state power having been abandoned as either impossible or undesirable. Among the broader Left, their condemnations of the liberals and social demo-crats in power pack little punch, because the Left does not have a viable political project to oppose to those whose sole aim is to put a slightly more human face on capitalism.

The key task for the Left is thus to develop a political project for transforming society in a fully democratic, egalitarian, and inclusive direction. In short, we need to revive the socialist alternative. As even the most hopeful examples—like Bolivia's indigenous-led revolutionary process—suggest, this will be a long, arduous, and contradictory process. The financial crisis and recession that began in 2008 may have dented capitalism's legitimacy, but there is no quick route to overcoming its global hegemony.

Well-worn hopeful slogans aside, we still need to convince both ourselves and the rest of society that politics can amount to more than selecting the least evil, and that a better world is indeed possible.

# ACKNOWLEDGMENTS

This book represents a collective effort, in the sense that it is informed by the incredible people with whom I work for peace and social justice. It is hard for an activist to steal enough time to write; I hope this work will justify the theft and prove of some use to our great collective struggle to change the world for the better.

Charles Demers has been a dear friend and my closest intellectual collaborator—I cannot thank him enough for his support in bringing this project to completion. My thanks also to the always courteous and skilled editorial team at Verso, including Tom Penn, Andrea D'Cruz and Mark Martin. Thanks are due as well to Tariq Ali—a great inspiration and teacher to generations of activists—for encouraging me to pursue this subject.

Special thanks to my mother Catherine—on top of everything else she is a talented writer and a supportive and helpful editor. Her decency, curiosity and sense of fairness—like that of my father David and my late grandparents, Beth and Gordon—has shaped my outlook on life.

Finally, I want to express my endless love and gratitude to Andrea Pinochet-Escudero, my compañera, best friend, and the mother of our little Gabriel. May he inherit a less evil world.

# LIST OF ABBREVIATIONS FOR BOOKS
# BY MICHAEL IGNATIEFF

| | |
|---|---|
| BB | *Blood and Belonging* |
| CJF | *Charlie Johnson in the Flames* |
| EL | *Empire Lite* |
| IB | *Isaiah Berlin: A Life* |
| LE | *The Lesser Evil* |
| RA | *The Russian Album* |
| RR | *The Rights Revolution* |
| TPL | *True Patriot Love* |
| VW | *Virtual War* |
| WH | *The Warrior's Honour* |

# NOTES

## PREFACE

1 Al Purdy, "Small Wars," from the collection *The Stone Bird*, McLelland and Stewart, 1981, p. 53.

2 Ron Graham, "The Stranger Within," *The Walrus*, January/February 2010.

## INTRODUCTION

1 Michael Valpy, "Being Michael Ignatieff," *Globe and Mail*, August 26, 2006.

2 Conor Gearty, "With a Little Help From Our Friends," *Index on Censorship*, February, 2005

3 Richard Seymour's *The Liberal Defence of Murder* (Verso, 2008) contains a comprehensive demolition of "liberal" and "left" apologists for imperial violence, past and present. The late Tony Judt named Ignatieff in a scathing article denouncing "Bush's useful idiots" (September 21, 2006, London Review of Books).

## 1 THE SOLIPSISTIC COSMOPOLITAN

1 Eric Hobsbawm, *Uncommon People*, New Press, 1998, p. 298.

2 As quoted in the Introduction to Canadian writer Tom Wayman's *A Country Not Considered* (House of Anansi, 1993).

3 "Michael Ignatieff et ses sourcils à Infoman," available at www.youtube.com

4   Writing in the Canadian online publication *TheTyee.ca*, Richard Warnica nailed the solipsistic focus: "In a 30-year career as reviewer, reporter, essayist and commentator, Ignatieff established himself as one of the most prolific highbrow writers of his generation. Ignatieff has written well over 100 long features of one form or another for non-academic journals since 1976. Their scope and range is remarkably wide. But read together they tell a single story, the story of Michael Ignatieff" ("Reading Michael Ignatieff", November 27, 2006, available at http://thetyee.ca).

5   This is how French journalist Pierre Pean, in his polemical biography *Le Monde Selon K* (Fayard, 2009), sums up France's humanitarian warrior *par excellence* Bernard Kouchner's favorite method of argument.

6   Anyone who reads Fisk's epic 1200-plus page book *The Great War For Civilisation: The Conquest of the Middle East* (Fourth Estate, 2005) will be amazed that the author lived to tell some of his tales. One particularly harrowing scene recounts Fisk's time in a tent in Afghanistan with Osama Bin Laden and some of his lieutenants. Before he could conduct his interview, Fisk had to figure a way to decline Bin Laden's offer of "conversion" to Islam without making the Al-Qaeda leader feel he had lost face.

7   Rick Salutin, "Narcissieff in the Mirror of Politics," *Globe and Mail*, September 24, 2009, available at www.theglobeandmail.com

8   David Harvey, *Cosmopolitanism and the Geographies of Freedom*, Columbia University Press, 2009, pp. 80–1.

9   This includes the veteran Canadian journalist Peter C. Newman, who wrote a two-volume study on *The Canadian Establishment* (1975, 1981).

10   Valpy, "Being Michael Ignatieff." The hard-hitting piece made waves when it was published in 2006. Ignatieff makes a fascinating preemptive confession at the beginning of a sit-down interview with Valpy: "I think there are people who would say I've been very ruthless in my life. I am someone who has worried greatly about the price my ruthlessness has inflicted on others. I have worried about that. I do worry about that."

11   He developed his thesis into the book *A Just Measure of Pain: The Penitentiary in the Industrial Revolution 1750–1850* (Palgrave Macmillan, 1979).

12  Ron Graham, "The Stranger Within," *The Walrus*, January/February 2010.

13  Quoted by Josée Legault, "Just When You Thought Ignatieff's Troubles Couldn't Get Worse," available at www.vigile.net

14  See Murray Dobbin, "A Message for the Pre-election NDP," January 31, 2011, available at http://rabble.ca

15  "Ignatieff: Reporter-turned-politician," *Toronto Star*, December 29, 2010.

## 2 THE NEGATIVES OF LIBERALISM

1  Taylor's essay, "History Workshop Journal," can be read at the Making History website, www.history.ac.uk

2  Ibid.

3  Istvan Hont and Michael Ignatieff, eds., *Wealth and Virtue: The Shaping of Political Economy in the Scottish Enlightenment*, Cambridge University Press, 1986, p. 2.

4  Valpy, "Being Michael Ignatieff."

5  Christopher Hitchens, "Moderation or Death," *London Review of Books*, November 26, 1998.

## 3 BALKAN WARRIOR

1  "Kosovo Peace Accord," *Z Magazine*, July 2009.

2  Speech to the Chicago Economic Club, April 22, 1999 (full text available at www.pbs.org).

3  Denis Smith, *Ignatieff's World*, Lorimer, 2006, p. 49.

## 4 EMPIRE'S HANDMAIDEN IN IRAQ

1  From a book review by Misha Glenny in the *Guardian*, September 6, 2003.

2  Associated Press, "NATO to cut troop levels in Kosovo," December 16, 2009.

3  This became the catchphrase *du jour* early on in Barack Obama's presidency when he needed to explain away his administration's failure to prosecute Bush, Rumsfeld, Cheney et al. for war crimes. I don't know which was more shocking, that a lawyer would invoke such a facile mantra or that the press corps largely failed to question it.

4   Michael Ignatieff, "It's War, But it Doesn't Have to be Dirty," *Guardian*, October 1, 2001.

5   Christopher Hitchens, "Don't Commemorate 9/11," Slate.com, September 8, 2003.

6   Richard A. Clarke, *Against All Enemies: Inside America's War on Terror*, Free Press, 2004.

7   Ignatieff's full essay, "The American Empire; The Burden," is available at www.nytimes.com

8   "A Conversation with Noam Chomsky: Telling the Truth about Imperialism," interview by David Barsamian, *International Socialist Review*, 32, November–December 2003, available at www.isreview.org

9   Ibid.

10   See Noam Chomsky, *Failed States*, Allen & Unwin, 2006.

11   Lewis Lapham, "Light in the Window," *Harper's* Notebook, March 2003.

12   The letter was published in *Harper's* May 2003 issue.

13   *Queen's Quarterly*, Winter 2004 (p. 494).

14   Michael Ignatieff, "Lesser Evils," *New York Times Magazine*, May 2, 2004.

15   Laurie Taylor, "No More Mr Nice Guy," *New Humanist*, September–October 2005, available at http://newhumanist.org.uk

16   CanWest News Service, "Natynczyk Promotion to CDS Popular with U.S. Commanders," June 6, 2008, available at www.canada.com

17   This letter appeared in the *WSJ*, March 28, 2003.

18   CTV News, "Most Canadians Support War, Harper Tells US TV," April 4, 2003, available at www.ctv.ca

19   "Prepared Text of John Howard's Address on Iraq to the National Press Club," AustralianPolitics.com, March 13, 2003.

20   "Text of 2003 Stephen Harper speech," *Toronto Star*, September 30, 2008.

21   CTV News, "Harper Appears to Change Stance on War," June 9, 2004, available at www.ctv.ca

22   CBC News, "Harper Staffer Quits over Plagiarized 2003 Speech On Iraq," September 30, 2008, available at www.cbc.ca

23   CTV News, "Iraq War a Mistake, Harper Admits," October 3, 2008, available at www.ctv.ca

24   Michael Ignatieff, "Why Are We In Iraq? (And Liberia? And Afghanistan?)," *New York Times Magazine*, September 7, 2003, available at www.nytimes.com

## 5 DON'T TALK ABOUT PALESTINE

1   Michael Ignatieff, "Israel Apartheid Week and CUPE Ontario's anti-Israel posturing should be condemned," *National Post*, March 5, 2009.

2   "Statement by Michael Ignatieff on the Issue of Anti-Semitism & Intolerance," Liberal.ca, March 1, 2010.

3   Desmond Tutu, "Of Occupation and Apartheid," Counterpunch.org, October 17, 2002.

4   "Lesser Evils: Facing Terror in Israel and the United States," *Queen's Quarterly*, p. 498, December 22, 2004.

5   Ibid., p. 499.

6   Michael Ignatieff, "Why Bush Must Send In His Troops," *Guardian*, April 19, 2002.

7   Ibid.

8   CTV News, "Ignatieff Admits Gaffe over Mideast Conflict," August 10, 2006, available at www.ctv.ca

9   Radio-Canada's "*Tout le monde en parle*" (Everybody's talking about it), October 8, 2006.

10   Rob Duffy, "Ignatieff Haunted by Israel Remark," *The Varsity*, October 16, 2006, available at http://thevarsity.ca

11   "Good Looks, Nobel Lineage, Spineless," *Toronto Star*, December 16, 2008.

12   Liberal.ca, January 3, 2009.

13   January 8, 2009, *The Toronto Star*, "Ignatieff Says Israel Must Be Allowed to Defend Itself."

14   *The Toronto Star*, April 14, 2008, "Ignatieff Apologizes for Israeli War Crime Comment."

## 6 STAYING THE COURSE IN AFGHANISTAN

1   Thomas Walkom, "Don't Worry. He's the Same Old Harper," *Toronto Star*, January 8, 2011.

2   Caroline Lees, "Oil Barons Court Taliban in Texas," *Sunday Telegraph*, December 14, 1997.

3   Michael Neumann, "Michael Ignatieff: Apostle of He-manitarianism", Counterpunch.org, December 8, 2003.

4   In 2005, Human Rights Watch published the report "Blood-stained Hands," detailing the crimes of Afghanistan's warlords and strongly questioning their continued empowerment in the NATO-backed Karzai government. It's the sort of report one might have expected to be written by the director of an academic center for human rights policy. The full report is available at www.hrw.org

5   In fact, Hamid Karzai, as a minor tribal chief, originally supported the Taliban in the early 1990s.

6   "Brother of Afghan Leader Said to Be Paid by CIA," *New York Times*, October 27, 2009.

7   Afghanistan mineral wealth is estimated at over one trillion dollars. Canada is a world mining superpower.

8   "Challenges to Unity Many, Ignatieff Says," *London Free Press*, May 20, 2006.

9   CBC News, "Harper Unveils New Afghan Motion with 2011 End Date," February 21, 2008, available at www.cbc.ca

10  From the Empire Club's website: www.empireclub.org

11  The full speech can be read at http://speeches.empireclub.org

12  Count Nicholas' rather dull speech on the topic of youth and Canada is also available at http://speeches.empireclub.org

13  Michael Ignatieff, "Canada in the World," Empire Club, June 15, 2010.

14  Chantal Hébert, "Ignatieff, Rae Help Harper with the Conservative Base," *Toronto Star*, November 17, 2010.

## 7 THE LAST INVASION

1   Quoted in Susan Delacourt, "Ignatieff: Reporter-turned-Politician," December 29, 2010, available at www.thestar.com

2   Linda McQuaig, "Long on Mea, Short on Culpa," *Toronto Star*, September 10, 2007.

3   Michael Ignatieff, "Getting Iraq Wrong," *New York Times Magazine*, August 5, 2007, available at www.nytimes.com

4   Judith Miller, "Iraqi Dissidents Reassured in a Talk with Bush About the Post-Hussein Era," *New York Times*, January 12, 2003.

5   McQuaig, "Long on Mea, Short on Culpa."

6   Adam Gopnik, "The Return of the Native," *The New Yorker*, September 7, 2009.

7   Charlie Smith, "Michael Ignatieff Puts a Liberal Shine on the Canada Line," *The Georgia Straight*, September 6, 2009.

8   Video: "Tar Sands - Michael Ignatieff YLC Event Part 4," available at www.youtube.com/watch?v=/9XT1om6Kc1A

9   "Dion's Carbon Tax Plan Was a Vote Loser, Ignatieff Says," *Toronto Star*, February 28, 2009.

10  Robert Kunzig, "The Canadian Oil Boom," *National Geographic*, March 2009.

11  Valpy, "Being Michael Ignatieff."

12  Chantal Hébert, "Why Quebec is Loving Jack, Leaving Gilles," *Toronto Star*, April 23, 2011.